TABLE OF CONTENTS

PREFACE

Karen Gautney, M.S.

AAMFT Deputy Executive Director

If you look to an ethical code for definitive answers to each and every ethical dilemma, you will likely be disappointed. The *AAMFT Code of Ethics* is no exception. You will find relatively few absolute dos and don'ts, and no lists of prescribed actions for each possible case. There are simply too many variables in human relationships, intentions, and perceptions to write an ethical guide that way. Instead, an ethical code offers some general principles, ethical ideals we can aspire to, some guidelines for action, and some prohibitions.

Ethical decision making is a journey. Along this journey we find fences that we may not cross, lest we are clearly in violation of ethical principles. The prohibition against sex with clients (*AAMFT Code of Ethics*, Principle 1.4), and the requirement to obtain written consent before taping clients (Principle 1.12) are two such fences. Laws and legal precedents also offer stern warnings about actions to be avoided.

At the same time, our path is illuminated by the aspirations and general guidelines found in the *Code*. We are extolled, for example, to respect and guard the confidences of clients (Principle II), and admonished to avoid exploiting the trust and dependency of clients (Principle 1.3). These aspirations assume that the therapist is interested in doing the right thing, and will apply good faith and common sense in the pursuit of ethical practice. Staying abreast of best practices and clinical research is a step in this direction.

Even with the prohibitions and aspirations offered by the *AAMFT Code of Ethics*, the therapist must identify relational flagstones on the ethical path. These include further guidelines, taken in context of other guidelines, from the *AAMFT Code of Ethics*. For example, the principle of non-discrimination (1.1) must be applied in respectful consideration of the client's best interest (1.9 and 1.10). The systemic thinker is well equipped to consider these relationships between ethical principles as well as the perspectives of the multiple parties in family therapy, given that a violation is often what is *perceived* by another as inappropriate, not what was *intended* by the therapist. Continuing study of therapeutic ethics can assist in recognizing relationships and multiple perspectives, as can clinical supervision or consultation.

So, combining the aspirations and guidance offered by the *AAMFT Code of Ethics*, the desire to do the right thing, laws and legal precedents, what we know of best practices, clinical supervision, and common sense will generally make the ethical path clear in even the most complicated situations. The *Code* must be applied in the context of all these things, and this *User's Guide* is a tool to help the clinician learn to do just that.

We have assumed that readers are concerned with ethical practice and are unlikely to commit blatant ethical violations; therefore, examples of the most obvious violations would offer little learning opportunity. Thus, the scenarios you will find in this book are not necessarily de facto ethical violations. They are constructed to show the complexity of possible situations in which well-meaning therapists can find themselves. Examining how the hypothetical situation developed, where the mistakes were made, and deciding what to do next, will help therapists avoid such missteps in their own practice.

We are indebted to the chapter authors for lending their time and expertise to this project. My thanks go also to Lincoln Stanley, an AAMFT ethics case manager who organized the content of this book, put together this who's who of ethics experts to serve as authors, and edited the final product. We hope that this *User's Guide* will assist you in applying the *AAMFT Code of Ethics* to your everyday practice.

Introduction to 2001 AAMFT Code of Ethics

Alan J. Hovestadt, Ed.D.

Development of the 2001 Code of Ethics was initiated as a result of a recommendation made by AAMFT President-Elect, Anna Beth Benningfield and President, Anthony Jurich to the AAMFT Board of Directors in August 1998. They proposed that a task force be created to review the then-current <u>Code of Ethics</u> and to offer recommendations for revisions to the Board of Directors. In October of 1998, the Board voted to create the Task Force on the Code of Ethics Review, appointing Alan J. Hovestadt as chairperson for 1999–2000. The Board of Directors appointed a diverse task force of distinguished AAMFT members representing multiple work settings and broad knowledge of issues related to ethics and Code enforcement in different arenas. Appointed were Thomas E. Clark, Maria T. Flores, Patrick W. O'Malley, Marlene F. Watson, and Robert H. Woody.

The AAMFT Board of Directors charged the task force to address modifications needed to clarify, update or expand the Code to be congruent with practice, training, and research environments for marriage and family therapists today and into the 21st century. The Board did not ask for an entirely new Code because surveys of AAMFT members indicated broad satisfaction with most aspects of the then-current Code. The charge to the task force, in accord with the AAMFT Strategic Plan adopted in July 1998, was that recommendations come in the form of an enforceable Code that could be included in state or provincial statutes or rules that locally regulate the profession of marriage and family therapy. In addition to having an enforceable Code, the Board, based on its Strategic Plan, desired to bring about greater alignment between AAMFT standards and regulatory board standards. The Board wanted the new Code to be one that could be advocated for and easily implemented by regulatory bodies.

During two years of study, deliberation, and writing, the task force was assisted by several AAMFT staff members, including but not limited to Lincoln M. Stanley, Ethics Case Manager; Marjorie Brown, Associate General Counsel; Celeste B. Zbikowski, Professional Standards Specialist; Paul Saunders, Associate General Counsel; and John P. Ambrose, former Director of Legal and Governmental Affairs.

During 1999 and 2000, the task force sought and received input from the membership of AAMFT, divisional presidents, members of all governance units and sub-units within the Association, the Board of Directors, state and provincial regulatory bodies, and consumers. Opportunities for input were announced through Family Therapy News, the DivList for Divisional Presidents, a program at the 1999 annual conference, and reports from the AAMFT President to divisional leaders. Illustrative of widespread interest in the proposed Code revisions was that more than 125 feedback items were received, studied, and reviewed by the task force after the first draft of the proposed Code published in the October/November 1999 issue of Family Therapy News. All in all, more than 400 items of feedback were received from virtually every stakeholder group.

The task force met in person, or via telephone conference call, on four occasions during the years of 1999 and 2000. The task force submitted its proposed Code revisions to the AAMFT Board of Directors during the spring of 2000 with the first full Board review occurring at its April 2000 meeting. Final adoption occurred at the April 2001 Board meeting including the setting of July 1, 2001, as the effective implementation date for the new AAMFT Code of Ethics. The entire Code can be found in the appendix of this book, or it can be reviewed and downloaded at the AAMFT website (www.aamft.org).

While there is significant new and revised content in the 2001 AAMFT Code of Ethics, there is also a large measure of continuity reflecting basic concerns that define ethical principles intended to guide our practice as marriage and family therapists. The 2001 Code is intended to define that which could be labeled as normative conduct in the practice of our profession. Notwithstanding the continuity of our Code of Ethics, the 2001 Code makes explicit many ethical obligations that were implicit in the prior Code. Thus, therapist conduct and ethical considerations pertaining to such issues as client welfare, prohibitions about sexual intimacy, professional competence, due care, confidentiality, informed consent, and financial arrangements, continue to be represented in the new Code.

Following are several highlights of revisions found within the 2001 AAMFT Code of Ethics. MFTs' responsibility to clients is perhaps the most important tenet in ethical therapy, thus its prominence as the first principle addressed in the AAMFT Code of Ethics. The 2001 Code rephrases the anti-discrimination subprinciple (1.1) as an affirmative obligation, and expands the classes of people mentioned. Informed consent is emphasized and described (1.2).

The subprinciple on dual relationships was rephrased to emphasize the protection of clients. The concern is not the mere existence of a dual relationship, but the risk of the therapist's judgment being impaired, or the risk of the client being exploited. The prohibition against sexual intimacy with clients is emphasized (1.4), and there is still an absolute prohibition for two years following therapy. However, the 2001 Code rejects any notion that harm will not occur simply by letting a two-year period pass, and places the burden on the therapist to avoid exploitation no matter how much time has passed.

Other elements to highlight from this section include the concept that the therapist will continue seeing a client only so long as the client will benefit (1.7), and will appropriately refer any client the therapist cannot help (1.8).

Principle II focuses on a therapist's obligation to maintain confidentiality. Emphasis is placed on ensuring that clients understand possible limits to confidentiality (2.1). Subprinciple 2.2 removes a long-standing source of confusion by making it clear that written consent is required for therapists to disclose individual confidences to others within the unit of treatment. Also, therapists are prompted to think ahead as to how confidentiality will be maintained upon closing a practice or the death of the therapist, as well as when storing and transferring records (2.5). When consulting with colleagues or referral sources, therapists are cautioned to protect client identity unless permitted, and limit disclosures to what is clinically necessary (2.6).

Principle III discusses professional competence and integrity. The new Code emphasizes that therapists should not practice new techniques or specialties without proper education and supervision (3.6), and reminds therapists that there is an ethical obligation to stay abreast of developments in the field (3.5).

Principle IV addresses the therapist's responsibilities to students and supervisees. To emphasize the prohibition of providing therapy to students and supervisees (4.2) and against sexual intimacy with students and supervisees (4.3), the 2001 Code makes these statements separate subprinciples. It goes further in prohibiting the acceptance of students and supervisees with whom the supervisor has a prior or existing relationship which could compromise the supervisor's objectivity (4.5).

Responsibility to research participants is the subject of Principle V, which had only minor editorial changes in revision of the Code. As is the theme throughout the Code, informed consent and protection of the research subject is emphasized.

Principle VI addresses responsibility to the profession. It provides guidance to employees when their organizational requirements conflict with the Code (6.1).

Specifically, the therapist is obliged to notify the employer of the conflict and his/ her desire to abide by the Code, and to make every effort to resolve the conflict in a way that adheres to the Code. This section of the Code emphasizes that therapists do not plagiarize or fail to cite authorship when due (6.3 and 6.4).

Principle VII focuses on financial arrangements, another area often overlooked. This issue is important to clients. Perhaps most important is ensuring that clients are well informed about what therapy will cost, and what will happen if the client becomes unable or unwilling to pay for services (7.2). For example, therapists generally cannot withhold records solely because payment has not been received (7.6). In an age when creative moneymaking is encouraged, therapists are prohibited from receiving payment for referrals (7.1), and must tread carefully if entering a bartering situation (7.5).

Those familiar with the earlier version of the AAMFT Code of Ethics will notice that Principle VIII, which addresses advertising by MFTs, is streamlined in the new version. The basic notion here is that advertising should be honest and not misleading. Clearly, competent practice must include significant attention toward the application of the AAMFT Code of Ethics within clinical practice. It is hoped that through reading this monograph, member discussions of ethical principles should strive to move beyond a recitation of do's and don'ts, to an understanding of how ethical principles can affirmatively guide one's own practice.

COMMENTS ON PREAMBLE

The Preamble of the 2001 AAMFT Code of Ethics provides overarching guiding principles of normative ethical practice for marriage and family therapists. Professional expectations delineated in these standards of conduct are enforced by the AAMFT Ethics Committee. While the 2001 AAMFT Code of Ethics attempts to be more explicit about duties and expectations of MFT's, no Code can cover every context, situation, or variable. Thus, the new Code advises members that the present standards are not exhaustive. Thus, members who are unclear or uncertain about issues or behaviors are encouraged to seek counsel of consultants, attorneys, supervisors, colleagues, or other appropriate authorities.

Other elements of the Preamble worth highlighting include situations where the AAMFT Code of Ethics prescribes a higher standard than required by law. In these instances, MFT's must meet the higher standard of the AAMFT Code. Situations may occur when laws and the Code are in conflict. In these situations, the new Code mandates that MFT's make known their commitment to the AAMFT Code of Ethics and take steps to resolve the conflict.

Other features in the Preamble inform members that the Code of Ethics is binding on all members of AAMFT, including all membership categories. We have an obligation to be aware of all aspects of the Code, and ignorance of or misunderstanding of standards of ethical conduct, are not legitimate defenses to a charge of unethical conduct. The final paragraph of the Preamble provides explanatory comments regarding the AAMFT's ethics complaint process and reminds accused persons that they are considered innocent until proven guilty and are entitled to due process.

PRINCIPLE 1: SUBPRINCIPLES 1.1 THROUGH 1.6
RESPONSIBILITY TO CLIENTS

1

Gregory Brock, Ph.D.

Serving clients' needs and protecting their interests is the foundation on which the integrity of the profession of marriage and family therapy rests. It is no accident that responsibility to clients comes first among the eight principles making up the AAMFT Code of Ethics.

PRINCIPLE I RESPONSIBILITY TO CLIENTS

Marriage and family therapists advance the welfare of families and individuals. They respect the rights of those persons seeking their assistance, and make reasonable efforts to ensure that their services are used appropriately.

1.1 Marriage and family therapists provide professional assistance to persons without discrimination on the basis of race, age, ethnicity, socioeconomic status, disability, gender, health status, religion, national origin, or sexual orientation.

VIGNETTE: An MFT was newly hired by a family therapy agency where clients were allocated to clinicians through a centralized intake procedure. As the only African American therapist on staff, this therapist's caseload was comprised of all of the African American couples and families based on the long-standing notion that these clients would feel more comfortable with an African American MFT. At a staff meeting, the therapist raised a concern about this practice since it had mandated a waiting list for these clients. The therapist was told by the director, who was also the supervisor, that clients' needs came first and that the policy would remain in effect. Other staff agreed. They said they would not see African American clients because those clients were best served by an African American therapist. The therapist resigned and filed a complaint with the State Civil Rights Board, the state Regulatory Board and the AAMFT Ethics Committee.

COMMENTS: Discrimination takes many forms and as mental health service providers, MFTs are responsible for recognizing, avoiding, and changing both blatant and de facto discrimination practices. In this instance, the intentions of agency staff and administrators created a situation where some clients were wait-listed (deprived of services) because of their race. Underlying this intent were the racist and unfounded assumptions that all clients prefer a therapist of the same race and that client preference for the race of their therapist is the most important criterion in predicting case outcome.

1.2 Marriage and family therapists obtain appropriate informed consent to therapy or related procedures as early as feasible in the therapeutic relationship, and use language that is reasonably understandable to clients. The content of informed consent may vary depending upon the client and treatment plan; however, informed consent generally necessitates that the client: (a) has the capacity to consent; (b) has been adequately informed of significant information concerning treatment processes and procedures; (c) has been adequately informed of potential risks and benefits of treatments for which generally recognized standards do not yet exist; (d) has freely and without undue influence expressed consent; and (e) has provided consent that is appropriately documented. When persons, due to age or mental status, are legally incapable of giving informed consent, marriage and family therapists obtain informed permission from a legally authorized person, if such substitute consent is legally permissible.

VIGNETTE (a, e): A divorced parent called a therapist for help with a middle school aged child. In the initial session, the parent complained about different rules in the ex-spouse's home and that the child returned from visitations acting disrespectfully and actively fighting any request to help around the home. The parent signed a therapy agreement and said the custody arrangement permitted either parent to seek medical treatment for the child. After a second session, the therapist decided to see the child alone for several sessions to learn the child's view of the relationship between the parents.

When the child told the ex-spouse about the therapy sessions, this person called the therapist and asserted that the child was not to be seen alone or with anyone else. The ex-spouse stated that custody was not joint, that the therapist had improperly seen the child without the proper permission, and that a complaint would be lodged.

COMMENTS (a, e): In this instance, the therapist did not check to determine whether the initiating parent had the right to seek therapy either for or with the child. Best practice in this situation would have required a review of the actual divorce decree or other legal document that described the custody settlement, and keeping a file copy of that document. Engaging both adults in the therapy from the outset may also have resolved the custody question while involving them in the therapy process.

Some jurisdictions stipulate the number of sessions a minor may be seen without parental permission (typically only 1 or 2 and possibly only to determine the nature of the child's concerns; consult your local statutes). Also some jurisdictions permit minors to provide consent for very specific presenting problems (e.g., drug abuse, adolescent pregnancy, sex abuse).

VIGNETTE (b): A couple was in the second of six contracted sessions of treatment when their therapist stated that in two weeks they would need to spend the weekend on a retreat conducted by a colleague in the agency. For two weeks following the retreat, conjoint sessions would be suspended to permit them time to integrate new behaviors into their relationship. The couple was surprised and dismayed that they were not told of these arrangements when they began therapy. Their family life would not permit extended absence and they questioned the time off from sessions. They wondered whether the retreat and the lapse in treatment served as cover while their therapist handled some agency emergency or went on vacation or even entered drug abuse treatment, and they lodged a complaint.

COMMENTS (b): In determining whether a treatment will fit their needs, clients need to know what will happen over the course of treatment that may serve as a basis for rejecting the treatment. In this instance a change in the schedule prevented the couple from attending contracted sessions. Had they known of the changes, they may have sought another therapist.

VIGNETTE (c): After six months of work with a family in weekly sessions, the therapist concluded that the family was worse off as a direct result of treatment. All of the assessments showed a broad based deterioration in both family structure and process. This outcome was disappointing to the therapist who had invested in expensive training for a promising experimental treatment, hoping to nurture a struggling practice. Since the treatment was applied outside the awareness of the family members, no mention was made of it in the initial phase of therapy. The therapist decided that termination and referral was the best option and in accord with the method, revealed the treatment to the family. On learning of the subterfuge, the family rejected the therapist's plea for understanding and angrily stated they felt like guinea pigs. They left the final session with the expressed intent of filing a complaint.

COMMENTS (c): Before implementing an experimental treatment, a therapist must obtain the client's informed consent. This includes making the client aware of the experimental nature of the treatment and the potential risks associated with it as well as informing the client there may be unknown risks associated with the treatment.

When traditional treatments are used, the code does not require the disclosure of risks. Any such disclosing is at the therapist's discretion. Therapists may choose to ensure that clients possess the common-sense awareness that even successful therapy may involve unpredictable emotional discomfort and/or relational changes. Clients can be informed that although a treatment has been shown to be successful with others, there is no way to determine accurately beforehand that the treatment will be successful for them.

VIGNETTE (d): A client initiated sessions with an MFT to address symptoms of depression associated with a troubled 30-year marriage. The client and therapist worked together for eight sessions and established a close and effective working relationship. The therapist felt it was time for the client's spouse to join them in the next session. When the client stated they should wait, the therapist reluctantly agreed but stipulated that the spouse would need to join them by the tenth session or the therapist would refer the case to another practitioner. At the tenth session, the spouse appeared and complained bitterly that the client had threatened suicide unless the spouse submitted to conjoint treatment. Furthermore, while the spouse agreed to attend sessions out of fear for the client's well being, the spouse was very angry at both the client and the therapist, and stated the intent to complain to authorities.

COMMENTS (d): This is an example of how efforts to bring reluctant partners into therapy can extort cooperation rather than win it. Children especially can be victims of involuntary consent. Therapists must assess carefully the motives that bring their clients to therapy and ensure that consent is freely given out of a clearly perceived benefit from the treatment.

1.3 Marriage and family therapists are aware of their influential positions with respect to clients, and they avoid exploiting the trust and dependency of such persons. Therapists, therefore, make every effort to avoid conditions and multiple relationships with clients that could impair professional judgment or increase the risk of exploitation. Such relationships include, but are not limited to, business or close personal relationships with a client or the client's immediate family. When the risk of impairment or exploitation exists due to conditions or multiple roles, therapists take appropriate precautions.

VIGNETTE: An MFT was called by a client whose partner had become violent during a quarrel. An emergency session with the couple was scheduled for early the next morning. At the first meeting, the therapist noted but did not comment at the time that the partner was the postal worker who delivered the therapist's daily mail.

Following the initial session in which each partner was interviewed alone and conjointly and constructed a safety plan for the client, the therapist received no mail for several straight days. Repeated calls to the post office yielded no explanation. In the second session, the partner cataloged the many ways in which the client was inept. The thought crossed the therapist's mind that the partner had considerable influence over the therapist's daily life, even financial well being. Mail resumed after that session. The therapist spent time in the third session alone with the partner to deal with the mail delivery issue. The partner denied knowing anything, but the following day no mail was delivered. Irate, the therapist cancelled all sessions the next day and waited on the carrier's route intending to threaten a formal complaint. Again the partner denied withholding mail delivery, and a yelling match ensued. Neither the client nor the partner showed up for the next scheduled session, and the therapist heard nothing until a call from the State Regulatory Board revealed that the clients had filed a complaint. Meanwhile, the postmaster called the therapist to apologize for disrupted delivery due to a malfunctioning mail sorting machine.

COMMENTS: No overt relationship was joined between the therapist and the mail carrier (the partner); nonetheless, the therapist depended on the carrier for an important service. This dependency constituted a potential threat to the treatment that should have been recognized. Many of the therapist's clients were harmed by the therapist's failure to refer the partner to another therapist as soon as the relationshipwas known.

1.4 Sexual intimacy with clients is prohibited.

VIGNETTE: An MFT established deep and caring relationships with clients. Sessions often included touch, a pat on the arm or back, or a hug when initiated by the client. The therapist was careful to ask permission when touching a client the first time.

Jamie and Morgan entered therapy complaining of anger and frustration stemming from differences in their preferred modes of expressing affection sexually. They related that Jamie desired to engage in more public displays of sexuality that included rubbing against strangers while Morgan distracted them. Initially, Morgan cooperated with these episodes because when they were alone, Jamie was a more patient and caring lover. But over the past year, Morgan had refused to participate and all sexual relations between the couple had come to a halt. Both felt trapped and abused by the other.

In the initial session in which the partners openly expressed fear for their relationship, the therapist felt relaxed and strongly connected with the couple. Late in the session, Morgan broke down, sobbing for an extended time. The therapist waited for Jamie to offer nonverbal support and when it became clear that would not occur, the therapist moved close to Morgan and offered a hand to hold. Morgan latched on and held tightly, pulling the therapist close. Jamie exploded with a barrage of questions: How could Morgan be so openly expressive with a stranger? What did the therapist have that Jamie lacked? How could the therapist fall for Morgan's manipulations? With the last statement, Jamie abruptly left the session, slamming the door on the way out and promising to file a complaint.

COMMENTS: Sexual intimacy encompasses a broad range of behavior extending well beyond engaging in intercourse or touching a client's genitals. Pecks on the cheek, holding a client's hand, or light hugging may have sexual undertones with strong associations for clients. Therapist intent is important in determining whether sexual intimacy occurs, however, client perception is important as well.

In this case, the therapist engaged in a common practice (offering support by holding the client's hand) in an uncommon situation. The presenting problem should have alerted the therapist that touch would prove to be a trip wire every bit as evocative as more overt forms of sexual intimacy.

Touch is no small matter between therapist and client. Careful, documentable assessment must precede action. Sensitivity is required always and especially when presenting problems involve sexual abuse. Blanket assumptions that clients will perceive touch of any kind as non-sexual are not warranted.

Some therapists make it a practice not to touch clients beyond a handshake on meeting initially. That does not mean they are uncaring, cold, or unresponsive. It does mean they work to prevent misperceptions, and they strive to prevent the unwitting imposition on clients of their own needs for affiliation, affirmation, and affection.

1.5 Sexual intimacy with former clients is likely to be harmful and is therefore prohibited for two years following the termination of therapy or last professional contact. In an effort to avoid exploiting the trust and dependency of clients, marriage and family therapists should not engage in sexual intimacy with former clients after the two years following termination or last professional contact. Should therapists engage in sexual intimacy with former clients following two years after termination or last professional contact, the burden shifts to the therapist to demonstrate that there has been no exploitation or injury to the former client or to the client's immediate family.

VIGNETTE: A client worked alone with an MFT on marital issues related to depression. From the outset a sexual tension existed between them that was discussed openly. While therapy was ongoing, the therapist established a clear boundary that precluded sexual intimacy for at least two years after ending sessions. Therapy ended with the client deciding to separate.

Several years later, ex-client and therapist met at a party. The ex-client was still separated and all but divorced. They ended up spending the night talking together, and then became sexually intimate. A few days later the therapist decided that what the ex-client really wanted was to reestablish their therapy relationship. Unfortunately, that possibility was fraught with problems because they had become lovers. The therapist broke off the affair, and offered to recommend another therapist. The ex-client remarked that more therapy was not an answer.

Months later, the therapist happened onto the ex-client in a grocery store. They chatted briefly, and the ex-client related that things were not going well. The ex-client was under medication, had withdrawn socially, and once again was experiencing feelings of disconnectedness and panic, stating that the feelings had become more pronounced after the affair. The therapist offered another referral but was rebuffed. Fearing the worst, the therapist even offered to talk "informally" with the ex-client for "a few times" just to help a little with what the therapist called an "existential crisis." The ex-client refused and said that life wasn't bad enough to need any help from the therapist.

Realizing the seriousness of the ex-client's condition, the therapist sought consultation from a colleague. They decided that the colleague would contact the ex-client, despite the confidentiality breech, and offer free consultation or handle any short-term commitment procedures. Meanwhile, the therapist would report the affair to the Ethics Committee and stand up to any consequences.

COMMENTS: The therapist failed to exercise good judgment in becoming sexually involved with a former client despite the passing of the required minimum of two years since the last professional contact. The client, and possibly the client's spouse as well, were harmed by the affair.

With all past clients there is the possibility that they will seek to reestablish services with their prior therapist. When that option is closed because a non-therapeutic relationship has developed, the client suffers. In this instance had the therapist been wise enough to avoid becoming sexually involved, the outcome may have been very different. An attraction existed during therapy itself but was handled appropriately. The context for the after-therapy affair however was established within the therapy. As a result, no full resolution of the therapy relationship occurred even though an extended time had passed. It was the therapist's responsibility to protect the client and the client's family and to possibly never become romantically involved or to engage in any other type of relationship with this client.

1.6 Marriage and family therapists comply with applicable laws regarding the reporting of alleged unethical conduct.

VIGNETTE: In an initial session, an MFT learned that a new client couple, who had been seen by a previous therapist, were advised to end their relationship. The previous therapist had said the partners were conflict habituated and that since their violent episodes were escalating, separation was recommended along with divorce since the pattern was long-standing. On hearing this advice the couple ended the sessions with the previous therapist. Their religious convictions did not permit divorce, and separation would have been highly embarrassing in their religious community. After a month away from therapy, the couple decided to try working with a new therapist. As do many therapists who hear this story from clients, the new therapist wondered whether their allegation was true. The new therapist considered asking the couple's permission to contact the previous therapist to verify their claim but decided not to and let the matter drop.

In the second session the couple pressed the new therapist to say that their first therapist was wrong, and that they should stay together. The therapist refused. Little progress was made, and they failed to show for a third session. Several weeks later the new therapist was called by a reporter who was working on a story describing the couple's joint suicide. A note left behind had related how the couple had contacted their first therapist who had reasserted the need to divorce. Their note also stated that the new therapist had not supported their desire to remain together. The reporter asked why the new therapist had not reported the previous therapist as required by state law.

The new therapist was prosecuted for an ethics code violation under state law. On conviction, the Regulatory Board reported the case to AAMFT for action by the Ethics Committee.

COMMENTS: Both therapists lived in a state where reporting suspected ethics code violations by other therapists is mandated (this is true of all states where the American Association of Marriage and Family Therapy Regulatory Board's Model Code of Ethics is the statutory code). Where reporting is mandated, therapists must comply.

In this instance, a seemingly minor breech of the state code and the AAMFT Code had lethal consequences. The therapist should have made the couple aware that they could issue a complaint and that if they chose not to, the therapist would do so.

PRINCIPLE 1: SUBPRINCIPLES 1.7 THROUGH 1.13
RESPONSIBILITY TO CLIENTS

Marilyn Peterson Armour, Ph.D.

2

1.7 Marriage and family therapists do not use their professional relationships with clients to further their own interests.

VIGNETTE: Sandy, a respected and highly experienced MFT in private practice, received referrals from a variety of sources. Sandy's spouse Avery was recently licensed as a marriage and family therapist and trying to build a practice. Avery used Sandy's office to see clients. Sandy received a call from a referral source who was seeing a couple and wanted to refer the husband to Avery. The referral source believed that Avery has the maturity and confidence to be particularly helpful to this man who had recently been laid off work. Sandy concured and encouraged the referral. Avery began seeing the client. After six sessions, Avery got into a shouting match with the husband about the husband's refusal to actively search for employment. Shortly thereafter, Sandy received a call from the referral source who heard, from the couple, about the disastrous session.

COMMENTS: This subprinciple requires MFTs to be aware of their personal motivations in making decisions that impact clients. It is built on the premise that personal needs can cloud the clinician's ability to be objective and potentially impair the primacy of attention to the client's needs. In this example, Sandy consulted with the referral source about Avery's professional qualifications and agreed that a referral to Avery was appropriate. Sandy could not be certain that the assessment of Avery was objective because Avery was Sandy's spouse. Moreover, since Avery was newly licensed and trying to build a practice, it is probable that Sandy's opinion was influenced by a desire to help Avery get started. By using Sandy's office, Avery minimized expenses. Consequently, Sandy's support of the referral may also have been motivated by Sandy's concern for their joint financial situation.

While not the primary therapist for the client, Sandy may have been viewed as a kind of superior or "supervisor" in this case. The referral source contacted Sandy because of Sandy's reputation and expertise. Sandy advised the referral source to proceed in contacting Avery. When things blew up, the referral source again contacted Sandy. Because Avery worked out of Sandy's office, the perception could be that Sandy was responsible for the quality of Avery's work.

Family members who work together are vulnerable to improprieties. Consequently, strict operating boundaries must be enforced to monitor and maintain the division between personal and professional relationships. If Avery and Sandy had drawn up a formal contract that delineated the boundaries in their working relationship, Sandy might have been better prepared to respond to the request for guidance from the referral source. The referral source could have been told that Sandy was not available to comment on Avery because of the spousal relationship. Sandy may not have been objective in this situation and therefore, any encouragement may have been construed by others as a potential conflict of interest. Sandy might also have suggested that the referral source contact Avery directly with questions. Sandy could have also recommended two or three other therapists to the referral source.

1.8 Marriage and family therapists respect the rights of clients to make decisions and help them to understand the consequences of these decisions. Therapists clearly advise the clients that they have the responsibility to make decisions regarding relationships such as cohabitation, marriage, divorce, separation, reconciliation, custody, and visitation.

VIGNETTE: Murray and Carroll sought couples therapy from an MFT. The couple felt that one of Carroll's parents had a destructive influence on Carroll and Carroll's relationship with Murray. Although childhood memories were few, Carroll felt as though sexual abuse had occurred in childhood at the hands of this parent. Carroll wanted the clinician, who had the training and experience to treat sexual abuse issues including recovered memories, to help in the recovery of memories. The clinician felt that Carroll may have been abused but did not believe that it was expeditious to "hunt" for memories. "After all, the abuse, if it happened, would have occurred long ago and staying stuck in the past will not help you to live in the present." The clinician, therefore, persuaded Carroll to focus on current problems in the couple's relationship, and also recommended that Carroll have less contact with the parent in question because the parent seemed invasive and controlling of the couple's life. Carroll took the MFT's recommendation and told the parent that the therapist had advised that they not to have contact. "Therefore," said Carroll to the parent, "we won't be getting together in the future." Carroll's parent was furious and filed a complaint. The parent alleged that the therapist had exerted undue influence on a vulnerable client and that this influence was destructive to the family. The therapist was shocked by the allegation since only 'recommending' that Carroll have 'less' rather than no contact with the parent.

COMMENTS: This subprinciple requires MFT's to both respect client self-determination and to provide clients with the information to help them make informed choices. It further stipulates that MFT's inform clients that the clients are responsible for any decisions they make. In this example, the therapist unilaterally decided that the client should not pursue memories of possible childhood sexual abuse. In so doing, the therapist foreclosed any exploration and dismissed the client's concern. Instead of addressing the client's agenda, the therapist advised the client to have less contact with the client's parent. At the time the therapist made the recommendation, the therapist also did not remind the client of the client's responsibility for whatever decision was made. Consequently, the client made the therapist responsible for the decision. The client's parent probably felt controlled by the therapist's power over the client's decisions and threatened by the potential loss of the parent's adult child. The parent therefore amassed power over the therapist by making a complaint to the licensing board.

Mental health professionals have hotly debated the issue of memory retrieval. Instead of making a unilateral decision about not pursuing memories of possible childhood sexual abuse, the therapist could have helped the client make a more informed decision by providing the client with information about traumatic memories as well as issues about the reliability of childhood memory. Providing information would have met the requirement in the principle for helping clients understand the consequences of their decisions. Moreover, since there were existing issues in the relationship between the client and the client's parent, the therapist could have suggested that Carroll seek therapy for Carroll alone or for Carroll and Carroll's parent rather than advising the client to avoid issues by not seeing the parent.

1.19 Marriage and family therapists continue therapeutic relationships only so long as it is reasonably clear that clients are benefiting from the relationship.

VIGNETTE: Paige and Paige's child, Tyler, were in therapy with MFT Leslie. Paige was also a mental health professional who did one-session mental health assessments, for the court, of parents in child custody disputes. Toward the end of assessing a client, Paige learned that a client was also in therapy with Leslie. Paige completed the assessment and later asked several colleagues to review the work done to ensure that Paige's conclusions were unbiased and substantiated by facts. Paige reported the situation to Leslie. Leslie was upset and insisted that Paige should have stopped the assessment and called in someone else to do it. Leslie also maintained that Paige needed to contact the licensing board and report that Paige had engaged in a dual relationship with the client. Paige felt blamed by Leslie for the problematic situation. Paige wondered how Leslie could continue to do therapy with Paige and Tyler since Leslie was so angry. "Maybe Leslie won't agree with my assessment of the client. Maybe the client will be angry with me for my assessment and talk to Leslie about it. How can Leslie keep all that straight and continue to see both the client and me and Tyler?" When Paige raised these concerns with Leslie, Leslie indicated that the only problem was Paige who needed to "own" what had gone wrong. Leslie suggested they meet without Paige's child until this could be sorted through. Paige complied because the therapy was important to Paige. However, Paige left each session feeling that Paige and Leslie were in a tug of war over who had done what to whom. Ultimately, Paige decided to leave therapy because there was no way to resolve the issues between them.

COMMENTS: This subprinciple requires MFT's to discontinue those therapeutic relationships that do not benefit clients. It raises questions about 1) what is and is not beneficial, and 2) who will determine that the relationship is not beneficial. In this example, a dormant dual relationship was suddenly activated. Leslie and Paige became professional colleagues as well as therapist and client. The therapist did not recognize that continuing the relationship would be hurtful to the client. Indeed, Leslie probably interpreted Paige's pain as guilt for or defensiveness against recognizing Paige's error in clinical judgment. Moreover, Leslie dismissed Paige's concerns about Leslie seeing both Paige and the client Paige had assessed. Paige had to make the decision, therefore, to terminate the therapeutic relationship. Indeed, Paige was clearly not benefiting from continuing the therapy. As Leslie's client, Paige felt that Leslie became a supervisor who had the requisite knowledge and right to evaluate Paige's clinical judgment. When Paige raised appropriate questions about the triangle between Leslie, Paige, and the assessed client, Leslie dismissed Paige's concerns and left Paige alone to worry about the potential for ongoing problems. Finally, when Leslie told Paige to make a report to the licensing board, Paige felt blamed for circumstances beyond Paige's control. Indeed, Paige's efforts to ensure an unbiased report were not recognized by Leslie.

Some dual relationships are not predictable or avoidable. Resolution of problems usually results in a loss for one or more persons. In this example, Paige lost the therapist. It could be argued that Paige broke confidentiality by sharing the situation with Leslie. It could also be argued that not sharing the situation would have created a secret about the fact that client and therapist were then also colleagues who shared a client. This secret could also have infected the therapeutic relationship.

1.10 Marriage and family therapists assist persons in obtaining other therapeutic services if the therapist is unable or unwilling, for appropriate reasons, to provide professional help.

VIGNETTE: MFT Galen saw Shannon and Jesse for couples therapy. Shannon had been granted a leave of absence from work because of depression. Although Galen attempted to schedule sessions for the couple, Jesse's travel schedule made it difficult for Jesse to attend sessions. Galen usually ended up seeing Shannon alone. After several months of working together, Shannon decided to join Jesse when traveling, as a way to manage Shannon's depression. "I just feel worse when I'm left all alone." As a result, Galen could not establish any regularity or momentum in either the couples or individual therapy. Shannon continued to be depressed and reported no improvement. Shannon provided Galen with a request and release of information to enable Galen to send a progress report to Shannon's employer. Shannon had asked for an extended leave of absence. Galen reported that Shannon only attended sessions infrequently and that no real progress had been made. Consequently, Shannon received notification that leave and benefits would not be extended. Shannon was furious at what Galen had reported, and insisted that the real problem was the therapist's incompetence. Shannon also called Galen and demanded twice-weekly sessions in order to prove to Shannon's employer that Shannon was serious about therapy. Equally upset, Galen worried about a damaged reputation in the professional community as well as Shannon's possible misuse of therapy to get benefits. Galen warned the psychiatrist who had prescribed Shannon's antidepressants about Shannon's manipulation. Galen decided not to see Shannon. When Shannon asked for referrals, Galen refused to give any names. "Since the names would come from me, these therapists wouldn't have a chance. You'd just see them as incompetent too."

COMMENTS: This subprinciple recognizes that there are circumstances when the therapist may need to discontinue services to a client(s). However, the principle stipulates that the therapist must help clients obtain other therapeutic services. In this example, Galen was unwilling to continue giving therapy to Shannon because Galen suspected that Shannon was misusing therapy to obtain extended benefits. Although the decision to discontinue therapy may have been appropriate, Galen's refusal to give referrals left Shannon stranded. Galen's call to the psychiatrist may have also ostracized Shannon and increased Shannon's isolation. Galen's behavior with Shannon's employer was questionable as well. Although Shannon signed a release of information, Shannon probably did not expect Galen to report the infrequency of therapy sessions and Shannon's lack of progress. Rather than 'reporting' Shannon to the employer, Galen should have talked directly to Shannon about these concerns. Galen also should have talked with Shannon prior to sending the report. It is possible that Shannon might have revoked the consent to release information after being 'informed' of Galen's opinions. Talking together might also have given Galen and Shannon the opportunity to either discontinue therapy or refocus it in a more productive direction. Finally, Galen's anxiety to protect a good professional reputation may have been a stronger motivator to discontinue therapy than Shannon's possible misuse of the process. Preferably, Galen's motivations would have been examined in consultation with a supervisor before Galen made the decision to refuse services to Shannon.

1.11 Marriage and family therapists do not abandon or neglect clients in treatment without making reasonable arrangements for the continuation of such treatment.

VIGNETTE: Brook sought help from MFT Aden for Riley, Brook's 6-year old child. Brook was divorced and concerned that Riley was not making a good adjustment. "My former spouse only sees Riley occasionally. My child feels like an orphan." Brook further reported that Riley was angry, lashed out at Brook, and provoked fights with the children at school. Brook felt fortunate that Aden was willing to see Riley. Aden was an exceptional therapist and accepted only a handful of new clients each year. Brook was willing to pay any fee, change Riley's schedule, and miss important meetings in order to see Aden. Aden lived up to Brook's expectations. Riley flowered under Aden's guidance and Brook was given new skills for working with Riley at home. Brook terminated therapy feeling grateful and empowered. Brook understood from Aden that Brook and Riley could return at any time for more therapy. Six months later, Brook's former spouse moved in with a new partner. Riley again reacted with extreme anger and sleep disturbances. Brook called Aden for help. When the call was not returned, Brook left messages about what was happening to Riley. After two weeks of no response, Brook sent a letter describing the efforts to reach Aden. Brook asked if Aden had been offended in some way. When there was no response to the letter, Brook sent a final letter expressing anger and disappointment, and describing the difficulty in explaining Aden's behavior to Riley, and the similarity between Aden's actions and those of Brook's former spouse. Brook asked for referrals for Riley but received no response.

COMMENTS: This subprinciple highlights the therapist's commitment to the client. It creates a safety net so that clients can risk showing who they are or becoming dependent without being deserted, forgotten, or ignored. It further directs the therapist to make arrangements for the continuation of services if and when the therapist cannot attend to the client's needs. In this example, Brook formed a tight bond with Aden based on reputation, help with Riley, and the explicit understanding that Aden would be available in the future. When attempting to exercise the option of returning for more help, Aden was not available. Moreover, Aden's lack of response left Brook questioning if Brook was to blame for Aden's silence. Unfortunately, Aden's silence replicated the unpredictability and inconsistency of Brook's former spouse in responding to Riley's needs. Did Aden have a responsibility to respond to Brook? From Aden's perspective, Brook and Riley were former clients. It could be argued, therefore, that Aden's lack of response did not constitute abandonment or neglect. Moreover, since Brook and Riley were not current clients, Aden was under no obligation to make arrangements for the continuation of their therapy. It could be further argued, however, that the implicit contract between Aden and Brook and Riley was for additional services on an as-needed basis. Since Aden had agreed to that arrangement, Aden probably had some responsibility to respond to Brook and to provide referrals if unable to see Brook and Riley for additional therapy.

1.12 Marriage and family therapists obtain written informed consent from clients before videotaping, audiotaping, or permitting third-party observation.

VIGNETTE: Many years ago, MFT Whitney had a training program for mental health professionals doing feminist family therapy. Whitney would periodically bring in nationally recognized feminist family therapists to do training and interview live families. The families came from the caseloads of the professionals in the training program. The families were given a consent form that explained that the live session would be taped and would be used only for educational purposes. Dallas was a trainee in Whitney's program. On one occasion, Dallas invited a client couple to be interviewed by the national presenter. The interview was productive and Dallas received many helpful suggestions. Dallas terminated with the couple after seeing them for several more months. Fifteen years later, Dallas found out that Whitney was teaching at the university and using the tape of the couple in the family therapy course. Dallas was upset since one member of the couple worked for the university and might be recognized by someone in Whitney's classes. Dallas met with Whitney to discuss this concern. Whitney was surprised to find that one member of the couple worked at the university, but said, "Both members of the couple signed the consent form and I am only using the videotape for educational purposes. Besides, there was no date for when the consent would expire."

COMMENTS: This subprinciple allows MFT's to show to third parties what has occurred (or is occurring) in therapy provided the client gives written informed consent. Informed consent goes beyond simple permission. It rests on the premise that the professional has a duty to disclose to the client information that allows the client to make a reasonable decision regarding his or her participation in treatment or other endeavor. Drawing on Subprinciple 1.2 concerning informed consent for therapy, we can infer that complete informed consent for third-party viewing of clinical material would require that clients 1) have the capacity to consent; 2) have been adequately informed of significant information that would influence consent, including potential risks; 3) have freely and without undue influence expressed consent; and 4) have provided consent that is appropriately documented. The couple in this example was not apprised of the risks of signing a release with no expiration date or provision for renewal of the consent. They were therefore not given adequate information. Moreover, they were not advised that clients could revoke their consent at any time and for any reason with respect to future use of the material. While the couple was not aware that Whitney was showing the film, Dallas's concern for the anonymity of Dallas's clients was sufficient reason for Whitney to discontinue using it. Finally, Whitney was showing the film in a context not anticipated by the clients when they signed the waiver years before. They might have withheld consent if they knew that one day the film would be shown in their place of employment. A legalistic approach to this scenario might find it adequate that the clients had agreed to "educational use" for an unlimited time period. But Subprinciple 1.12's higher ethical standard implies that this significant shift in the use of the film undercuts the couple's original consent and therefore it cannot be assumed that the couple's interests were adequately protected in the current situation. To remedy this, Whitney would need to seek a renewed consent contract from the couple accepting use of the film in the new location, for a specified time, making it clear that either individual could withdraw permission at any time.

1.13 Marriage and family therapists, upon agreeing to provide services to a person or entity at the request of a third party, clarify, to the extent feasible and at the outset of the service, the nature of the relationship with each party and the limits of confidentiality.

VIGNETTE: The Presbytery asked a therapist to see two ministers who were having communication problems. "We have a senior minister who has made some poor decisions. Indeed, we have lost four staff because they can't get along with the minister. We have a new assistant minister who is Mexican American and we do not want to lose another person. Some members of the congregation, however, feel that the assistant minister is cold and unavailable. Would you see them to help them work out their communication difficulties?" Dell agreed to see the two ministers. At the first session, Dell told the ministers that everything they talked about would be kept confidential. The senior minister insisted that the assistant minister keep the content of the sessions confidential too. Four sessions were held. Dell realized that the problem was much larger than communication issues and included charges by the assistant minister that the senior minister commonly lied or distorted information and that the senior minister had also had inappropriate relationships with parishioners. When the Presbytery called for an update, Dell felt bound. Dell had not established clear contracts with the Presbytery about giving them information. Moreover, Dell had promised the ministers confidentiality.

COMMENTS: This subprinciple recognizes that MFT's provide services to others for third parties. In these relationships, boundaries are apt to become enmeshed since the third party has an investment in the services given to others. Indeed, it may be difficult for MFT's to delineate the primary client. This principle stipulates, therefore, that MFT's must clarify the nature of the relationship with each party as well as the limits of confidentiality. In this example, Dell ran into difficulties because the boundaries and expectations in each relationship were not clarified prior to beginning work with the ministers. Moreover, Dell's promise of confidentiality made it impossible for Dell to give any information back to the Presbytery who, in this case, was the primary client. In the future, Dell needs to ascertain what the Presbytery expects, when they expect it, what they intend to do with the information, and what they have told the referred parties about their expectations. Then Dell needs to clarify with the referred parties the nature of Dell's relationship with the Presbytery and the extent to which confidentiality can be promised. While limiting confidentiality may reduce the sharing of information, the setting of realistic boundaries protects the needs of all parties and allows Dell the flexibility to move between the third party and the referred parties. Moreover, having clear boundaries sets standards about what will and won't be allowed. Such standards can provide a sense of safety and security to others.

PRINCIPLE TWO: CONFIDENTIALITY

Ingeborg E. Haug, D.Min.

3

Professional ethical behavior begins with the recognition that even seemingly insignificant actions in the therapy context have the potential to help or harm clients. Therapists are therefore asked to be intentional in their behavior and to reflect on the possible unintended consequences of their planned actions. The Golden Rule is a good maxim to keep in mind, namely to treat clients as therapists would like to be treated themselves.

Confidentiality might be considered the foundation to establishing a safe and therapeutic relationship in which clients can openly confide their personal concerns without fear of public exposure. With notable exceptions, the right to confidentiality belongs to clients, and it is clients' prerogative to determine whether, when, with whom, and to what extent their communications with a therapist can be shared. When clients unanimously agree to a release of information, therapists may not refuse this request.

The ethical mandate to maintain confidentiality is so widely accepted that it is written into the ethics codes of all major mental health disciplines—psychiatry, psychology, social work, marriage and family therapy, mental health counseling, and psychiatric nursing. Confidentiality, however, is also protected by law. Most states that license or certify marriage and family therapists have clearly articulated confidentiality/private communication legislation. While these laws vary from state to state, they generally spell out (1) under which circumstances and to what extent therapists may breach confidentiality without the explicit consent of their clients, such as for communication with other health professionals or for bill collection and (2) under which circumstances they must do so, like reporting suspected child and elder abuse and neglect, protecting clients and others from bodily harm, or being issued a subpoena followed by a judicial ruling that overrides therapist–client privileged communication in legal proceedings. Therapists living in states that do not license MFTs do well to follow guidelines for other licensed mental health providers in their state.

The AAMFT Code of Ethics emphasizes in its Preamble that "both law and ethics govern the practice of marriage and family therapy. When making decisions regarding professional behavior, marriage and family therapists must consider the AAMFT Code of Ethics and applicable laws and regulations." Since ethical and legal considerations overlap in issues of confidentiality, it is crucial that therapists educate themselves about specific laws and regulations which impact their practices. Sources of further ethical and legal information are listed elsewhere in this book.

As in all aspects of clinical practice, it behooves clinicians to be proactive rather than reactive in establishing policies regarding confidentiality and informing clients of these. The AAMFT Code of Ethics assists by giving the following guidelines.

Principle II Confidentiality

Marriage and family therapists have unique confidentiality concerns because the client in a therapeutic relationship may be more than one person. Therapists respect and guard the confidences of each individual client.

Marriage and family therapists embrace a systemic orientation that views problems as embedded in and maintained by interpersonal interactions. The initial exclusive emphasis on interactional systems, however, has over the past 20 years given way to a recognition and re-integration of the role of the individual in family treatment. Accordingly, the rights of each individual to confidentiality are explicitly affirmed in this principle and further detailed in its Subprinciples.

2.1 Marriage and family therapists disclose to clients and other interested parties, as early as feasible in their professional contacts, the nature of confidentiality and possible limitations of the clients' right to confidentiality. Therapists review with clients the circumstances where confidential information may be legally required. Circumstances may necessitate repeated disclosures.

VIGNETTE: A reverend referred a congregant to a marriage and family therapist for services. Prior to the initial appointment, the congregant/client received by mail the therapist's policies and procedures/informed consent forms together with directions to the office. At the beginning of the first session, after the initial welcome, the therapist inquired whether there were any questions regarding office policies, specifically confidentiality. The client, eager to address the marital conflicts for which therapy was sought, signed the form without further questions. A week later the therapist had to change their appointment, and after several attempts at reaching the client in person, the therapist left a message on the client's answering machine at work. A few days later the therapist was dismayed to learn that, in the client's absence, a colleague had been authorized to receive and respond to the client's phone messages. The client was furious about the breach of confidentiality and angrily refused to return to therapy. A few days after the session, the therapist met the reverend in the street, who inquired how therapy with the client was progressing.

COMMENTS: A positive therapeutic relationship between clients and therapist has been shown to be indispensable for successful therapy. Many therapists decide to postpone addressing "housekeeping" issues, including confidentiality and limits to confidentiality, until the end of a first session when they have established a positive connection with their clients. They fear alienating clients and giving the erroneous message that policies, legalities, and caveats take precedent over the concerns that brought clients to seek help in the first place. This policy, however, might lead unsuspecting clients to reveal incriminating information without knowing the likely consequences, such as a report to state authorities in the case of suspected child abuse or neglect. The therapist's policy of mailing out policies and procedures forms prior to a first appointment circumvents this problem and maintains clients' autonomy concerning disclosures. It also satisfies the ethic code's admonishment to inform clients "as early as feasible" and minimally distracts from the purpose of the session. However, the therapist failed to include in the policies adopted and in discussions with the client how to handle more subtle potential breaches of confidentiality such as leaving messages on home or work voice mail, handling accidental meetings in public places such as the supermarket or in church, using faxes, e-mail or filing third party reimbursement claims. While it would be clinically unwise to list every possible ethical dilemma at the onset of therapy, therapists are well advised to proactively address those they are likely to encounter in their particular practice setting. Additionally, if the client continued in therapy and invited a spouse or partner to conjoint sessions, the therapist would need to reiterate the policies and procedures with that partner.

Modern technologies create unique confidentiality dilemmas. Many phones, for instance, store phone numbers and names of callers. Unauthorized persons such as office cleaning crews or, if the therapist answers calls from home, family members could have access to client information unless phone memory is cleared. In addition, therapists ought to be mindful of the fact that conversations on cell phones and by e-mail are not secure, and that files stored on a computer hard drive may become accessible to others who use the same computer, or when a computer needs servicing.

In conversation with the reverend, the therapist declined to divulge any information concerning the client without an explicit written release from the client naming the reverend as the recipient of information. It is prudent for therapists to anticipate such inquiries from other "interested parties" such as concerned family members, referral sources, courts, school systems, physicians, guardians ad litem in the case of minors or incapacitated adults, or insurance companies. Requests for information may be received by phone, fax, e-mail, or in person. Absent an explicit written release from clients, therapists may be well advised to have a standard response at the ready, such as being "unable to even acknowledge who is or isn't a client of mine." In the case of therapy mandated by a third party—court systems, schools, ethics boards, for example—therapists have to ascertain from all parties at the outset what information needs to be reported, with what frequency, and what information, if any, is considered confidential.

In the preceding vignette, even if the therapist had obtained a release from the client to speak with the reverend, the setting of this conversation in a public place with no guarantee of privacy would still prohibit a response. Conversations regarding clients in unsecured settings and professional "gossip" among colleagues outside of professional case conferences or supervision constitute careless and serious breaches of confidentiality. It is equally important that therapists educate their administrative staff and billing services in stringent confidentiality measures and soundproof offices so that others may not overhear calls to clients, let alone therapy sessions.

2.2 Marriage and family therapists do not disclose client confidences except by written authorization or waiver, or where mandated or permitted by law. Verbal authorization will not be sufficient except in emergency situations, unless prohibited by law. When providing couple, family or group treatment, the therapist does not disclose information outside the treatment context without a written authorization from each individual competent to execute a waiver. In the context of couple, family or group treatment, the therapist may not reveal any individual's confidences to others in the client unit without the prior written permission of that individual.

VIGNETTE: A marriage and family therapist ended a session with a couple. During the following week one of the partner's travel schedule necessitated a change in appointments. As the therapist looked through the appointment book, the partner stepped up from behind to look for openings in the schedule that might work for them.

COMMENTS: This uncomfortable situation occurs not infrequently when therapists schedule their own appointments at the end of sessions. The therapist is well advised to close the appointment book and explain to the partner that the information contained in the weekly planner includes clients' names and needs to remain confidential.

VIGNETTE: A 15-year old child whose parents were divorcing was referred to an MFT for exhibiting behavior problems related to the divorce. The child was sent to therapy by one parent. After an initial session together with the referring parent, the child refused parental involvement in therapy. Over the course of the following individual sessions, the child confided to the therapist a near-daily use of marijuana and alcohol, as well as dangerous risk-taking behaviors like driving while intoxicated. One day the other parent called the therapist angrily and stated that both parents did not consent to therapy. This parent accused the therapist of biasing the child toward the other parent, and demanded to be sent copies of the therapy records. The child vehemently rejected any contact with this parent and asked the therapist to promise not to reveal therapeutic confidences to either parent.

COMMENTS: Almost always, when therapists provide services to minors whose parents are married, the consent of one parent is sufficient for providing medical or mental health treatment. If the parents are separated or divorced and have joint custody, either parent may consent to treatment except in those cases where the divorce decree specifies which parent has the power to obtain psychological or psychiatric care for the children. Some state laws require this level of specificity when granting a divorce, and therapists need to inform themselves regarding their respective jurisdiction. In cases of sole custody only the parent who has sole custody may consent to therapy.

In order to act proactively when seeing minors with or without a parent, therapists must inquire at intake about the parents' marital status and, in the case of divorce, whether the parent requesting services has the right to authorize such treatment. One way to accomplish this with minimal disruption is to include those questions in the policies and procedures/informed consent form that therapists review with clients prior to their signing.

The therapist belatedly ascertained that this child's parents had joint custody and that the referring parent could indeed authorize mental health treatment. Since the referring parent had been seen in therapy with the child for the first session and therefore was part of "the treatment context," any release of information, including to the other parent, would have required the referring parent's signature. Whether the child's signature was legally needed depended on the state or province's laws.

The age when minors may exercise privilege varies from jurisdiction to jurisdiction. The age of consent to treatment and releasing one's own information is typically set at age 16 to 18. Some jurisdictions, however, set the age as low as 12–14 and others are silent on the issue. In case of silence, the age should safely be assumed to be 18. Ethical considerations and legalities, however, do not always overlap completely. While the law may not require the child's signature as a minor, the ethical imperative to protect clients' welfare and interests extends to all family members, including a 15-year old. Assuming the child is mentally competent, that child's consent to a release of records would ethically be required.

The AAMFT Ethics Committee has not set any explicit age at which a minor's signature is necessary to release confidential information. An informal inquiry by the author, however, indicates that marriage and family therapists commonly request the signatures of children, often as young as 9 or 10 years of age, who are able to write and able to comprehend what they are signing.

In the above vignette the non-consenting parent might insist that the only interest is in information about the child, not the other parent. In the absence of a signed waiver from the referring parent, however, and even if the child consents to a release of information, the therapist cannot "split the file" in order to extract information concerning only the child. The non-consenting parent might pursue the goal by legal means through court order, hoping for a judicial decision that overrides therapist–client confidentiality.

Therapists' ethical imperative to advance first and foremost clients' welfare comes again under scrutiny when considering the child's serious acting-out behavior. Daily substance abuse in a minor may be looked at as suicidal behavior, especially in the light of risk-taking behaviors that endanger not only the minor but also others. Therapists should seriously consider seeking peer and legal consultation to review their treatment plan and clinical interventions. If the child's behavior continues or escalates in spite of therapeutic interventions and the therapist deems the behavior to be actively suicidal and homicidal, then the exception of Principle 2.2 of the Code, "mandated by law," may be met, though the law must be checked. In order to protect a child's life, the therapist would be justified in informing the referring parent of the child's behavior without the child's consent. It is, of course, a matter of clinical skill how this situation is handled so that clients' welfare is maximized and the child's dignity and cooperation may be protected.

Marriage and family therapists may proactively set policies concerning minors' substance abuse. They could, for example, inform families, including minors, at the outset that the therapist will not keep from parents prolonged substance abuse by their children since the therapist interprets such abuse as suicidal and will need to take measures to protect the client. Such a policy risks, of course, that minors are not forthright in admitting their substance abuse. It does, however, increase informed consent to treatment and respects clients' autonomy.

VIGNETTE: A marriage and family therapist was seeing a family for therapy. One day, the therapist received a phone call from one spouse's individual therapist who wanted to coordinate that spouse's treatment. When the family therapist mentioned this request to the family, a 14-year old family member flatly refused to sign a release of information form, stating "I don't want anyone else to know my business." A few days later the spouse in question called the family therapist and stated, "I thought you ought to know what my therapist wanted to talk to you about: I have been having an affair and am not sure about continuing my marriage. I don't want you to mention anything about this in our sessions, though."

COMMENTS: Since the Ethics Code requires the written permission of all members in treatment prior to releasing information, the child's refusal prevents the therapist from communicating with the spouse's individual therapist. This situation reflects the possible disparity between ethical and legal stipulations, as mentioned above. While most therapists would grant a 14-year old the same ethical right to confidentiality and protection of their interests as adults, the law may or may not mandate this signature, depending on state statutes.

The information the spouse in question shared confidentially with the therapist had clinical implications for the continued treatment of the family. The therapist, however, was unable to use the information unless the spouse keeping the secret gave written consent to release that information. The therapist would still be able to speak individually with the secretive spouse to clarify what the consequences might be to the client, the family, and the therapy process if the client continued keeping intentions a secret. If, however, therapy became "stuck" due to the unaddressed parental conflicts, the therapist might need to defer further services. This situation requires therapists' clinical skill and exquisite attention to detail to avoid accidental breaches of individual confidences, and in order to protect both the family and the individual's rights and wellbeing.

2.3 Marriage and family therapists use client and/or clinical materials in teaching, writing, consulting, research, and public presentations only if a written waiver has been obtained in accordance with Subprinciple 2.2, or when appropriate steps have been taken to protect client identity and confidentiality.

VIGNETTE: A marriage and family therapist is working with cancer patients and their families. Family members are encouraged to draw and/or express themselves poetically in an effort to help them communicate and externalize their experience. The therapist has been asked to lead a workshop on this work for nursing staff at a major hospital in the city nearby and decides to illustrate the approach with clients' artwork. To protect confidentiality, the therapist removes all names from drawings and poems that would identify clients and uses fictional first names when discussing the clinical usefulness of the approach. One client's relative, however, is in the audience and while not identifying the work's creator, recognizes the family in the therapist's narrative. The relative is appalled to have the family's emotional experience discussed in public.

COMMENTS: The safest way to use client materials in a public forum is to receive explicit written permission from clients, stating the extent of the information to be released, as well as the purposes and time limitation of the permission. The therapist in this example opted instead to protect clients' confidentiality by removing identifying information from all artwork. In order to illustrate the approach, however, the therapist provided clinical detail without enough concealment. It is often difficult to adequately disguise clients' identity without losing clinical detail relevant to teaching, writing, consulting, or research. A test of adequate disguise may be to establish whether a person who knows the client well would not be able to identify the person when told of the case. The therapist clearly failed in the duty to protect clients' confidentiality.

2.4 Marriage and family therapists store, safeguard, and dispose of client records in ways that maintain confidentiality and are in accord with applicable laws and professional standards.

VIGNETTE: A marriage and family therapist needs to quickly end a session for an urgent restroom break. The client prepares to leave, but is slow in gathering personal belongings. The therapist, in physical distress, confirms the client's appointment the following week at the agreed-upon time, and asks the client to find the way out in the therapist's absence. When the therapist returns from the restroom the office is empty. The client's file, however, which had been placed on the desk, is nowhere to be found.

COMMENTS: The mandate to keeping client records safe and inaccessible to unauthorized persons at all times is unintentionally but carelessly violated in the above situation. No matter the physical discomfort, the therapist should have waited until the client left (and locked the office door during the subsequent absence) or taken the client file along, assuming that there were no other files lying around. Similar potential breaches due to carelessness occur when therapists leave files on their desk and keep their office doors open to a common hallway while they are out getting a cup of coffee, retrieving the mail, or attending to other matters, or when therapists leave files and/or audio/videotapes in their car, or when they return client phone calls or listen to client tapes in their homes with other family members present.

Once the breach of confidentiality occurred, the therapist in this case discussed with a supervisor how to proceed. It seemed highly likely that the client took the file. Should the therapist call the client and ask about it, thereby pointing out the loss of the file, including the confidential information it contained, and risking the client's outrage? Might the client initiate a complaint to authorities? Might the client have harbored such intentions to begin with and hoped to gain financially? What if the therapist remained silent and the client or a subsequent therapist later requested access to the file, possibly in an emergency? Since different jurisdictions have differing stipulations how long medical, including mental health records, have to be retained by health service providers, therapists need to consult their state laws. A time frame common in several states is seven years past termination and three years past the death of client or therapists. However, since the AAMFT Code has no time limits to investigating ethics complaints and since files may document important details, therapists are well advised to save client files indefinitely. Given these facts, the case of the missing file could possibly come back to haunt the therapist years later. In consultation with agency administrators, the therapist decided to seek legal counsel and was advised to document the incident and refrain from taking any further action at that time.

2.5 Subsequent to the therapist moving from the area, closing the practice, or upon the death of the therapist, a marriage and family therapist arranges for

the storage, transfer, or disposal of client records in ways that maintain confidentiality and safeguard the welfare of clients.

VIGNETTE: A marriage and family therapist is terminating employment at a mental health agency to work solely in private practice. The therapist packs up personal belongings and office files and hires a moving company. One of the movers, carrying a box of client files, stumbles and drops the box, and the contents spill out and blow down the street. Some of the papers are never retrieved.

COMMENTS: When therapists leave agency employment, it is important to remember that the original files of agency clients belong to the agency. With the agreement of agency administrators, therapists may copy files for their own records.

Any storage, transfer, or disposal of client records, whether original files, copies, or private notes, necessitates particular attention by therapists to be sure no breach of confidentiality occurs. The therapist was negligent in this duty by failing to securely seal the boxes containing client files. In a local move, it may be best practice to move these sensitive materials personally, if feasible.

Principle 2.5 also requires therapists to proactively communicate to office managers or to the executors of their estate how client files should be handled in the event of their death. As mentioned above (Principle 2.4), therapists need to inform themselves of the timeframe set by their jurisdiction regarding the length of time records need to be retained under these circumstances.

2.6 Marriage and family therapists, when consulting with colleagues or referral sources, do not share confidential information that could reasonably lead to the identification of a client, research participant, supervisee, or other person with whom they have a confidential relationship unless they have obtained the prior written consent of the client, research participant, supervisee, or other person with whom they have a confidential relationship. Information may be shared only to the extent necessary to achieve the purposes of the consultation.

VIGNETTE: A marriage and family therapist and an AAMFT Approved Supervisor provides consultation for a group of licensed marriage and family therapists in private practice. Therapists take turns presenting a brief synopsis of cases and segments of audiotaped client interviews. Only clients' first names are used during case conferences and clients sign a release form granting permission to be audiotaped for the purpose of supervision. One day a therapist presents a session of a couple dealing with severe financial problems. When the audiotape is turned on, the supervisor is dismayed to recognize the voices of neighbors. The supervisor asks that the tape be stopped and informs the therapist of the situation, suggesting that the therapist consult a supervisor colleague for supervision of this case.

COMMENTS: When consultations or supervision occur live or through audio or videotape, unique confidentiality concerns are raised which always require clients' prior written consent. As the above situation illustrates, it would be highly advisable for therapists to include the name of the consultant or supervisor in their release forms. Also, if other supervisees recognize a client from other contacts, they need to excuse themselves from discussions of the case. The same principle applies when therapists present videotapes at conferences and any participant recognizes one of the clients.

It is generally assumed that agencies provide continuing education and case conferences to their clinical staff and that clients give their consent to these policies when they request services at an agency. Agencies as well as therapists in private practice still would be well advised to include in their policies statement a clause like "in order to provide excellence in clinical services and in accordance with accepted professional behavior, we (I) participate in case consultations and supervision provided by _____. Every effort is made to protect client identities." It is the responsibility of supervisors to educate their supervisees to restrict case presentations to clinically necessary information and to eliminate tangential materials that could identify their clients.

PRINCIPLE 3: SUBPRINCIPLES 3.1 THROUGH 3.9
PROFESSIONAL COMPETENCE AND INTEGRITY

Lucille M. Romeo, Psy.D.

PRINCIPLE III MARRIAGE AND FAMILY THERAPISTS MAINTAIN HIGH STANDARDS OF PROFESSIONAL COMPETENCE AND INTEGRITY.

3.1 Marriage and Family Therapists pursue knowledge of new developments and maintain competence in marriage and family therapy through education, training, or supervised experience.

VIGNETTE: An MFT provided family therapy to a husband and wife and their three children. During therapy, the parents divorced. The mother contested the custody of the children stating that the father was an unfit parent. The mother's attorney subpoenaed the therapist to testify and assess the parenting abilities of each parent. The therapist agreed and testified that the mother was a more stable and effective parent than the father. The father and his attorney made a complaint to the AAMFT Ethics Committee alleging that the therapist made these statements based on a biased opinion toward the mother that did not take into consideration the father's rehabilitation and his improving parenting skills.

COMMENTS: The MFT violated this principle by testifying about parenting ability after having provided therapy to the family. The MFT neglected to adhere to a new state licensing board regulation that excludes MFT's from testifying in custody or divorce cases if they have provided therapy to the parents and/or their children. Typically, child custody testimony requires the therapist to render an opinion concerning the competency of the parents, and to do so is a conflict of interest. Therefore, a neutral evaluator who has not previously worked with any of the family members is assigned to provide an objective viewpoint, assess parenting ability, and make recommendations concerning custody. Also, testifying in a custody case may impair further work with the child if the aggrieved parent does not support the therapy due to a sense of betrayal or anger.

In this case, the MFT was negligent in keeping abreast of the new developments per the state licensing board. The regulation had been announced in newsletters from both the board and the therapist's AAMFT division. The therapist also did not acquire supervision or consultation from a colleague that may have prevented this harmful and egregious error in judgment and competence.

3.2 Marriage and family therapists maintain adequate knowledge of and adhere to applicable laws, ethics, and professional standards.

VIGNETTE: An MFT created a therapy website and offered online consultation, advice, and support to individuals who requested assistance. A 45-year old client who lived in another state and was experiencing relationship problems acquired advice and therapy from the therapist, stating that it was more convenient and affordable to acquire help via online sessions than to see a local therapist weekly. The client's psychiatrist was informed of this arrangement during a medication follow-up appointment. The psychiatrist, who questioned whether this was legally or ethically correct, requested an investigation by the state licensing board.

COMMENTS: The therapist violated this principle by providing advice and therapy online, either through ignorance of the law or willful violation of it as it is considered illegal to provide therapy in a state in which one is not licensed. Ethically, one has to question whether therapy online can be effective when the therapist is not able to see the person face-to-face, observe the body language, hear the tone of voice, or accurately assess the person's emotional functioning. Risks may occur in cases of crisis or emergency, especially if the client becomes suicidal and requires immediate intervention and help. Confidentiality may become an issue and a liability risk if the electronic message is forwarded to another e-mail address by mistake or is read unintentionally by another individual. Third party payment may become complicated. It is, therefore, important for the therapist to become knowledgeable about rules and guidelines regarding electronically transmitted consultation or therapy by consulting with the state licensing board or the AAMFT Ethics Committee prior to offering services online.

3.3 Marriage and family therapists seek appropriate professional assistance for their personal problems or conflicts that may impair work performance or clinical judgment.

VIGNETTE: An MFT, who was also a recovering alcoholic, experienced a relapse after suffering several losses within a year's time: the deaths of a child and a parent. Due to increased drinking, the therapist arrived late for client appointments and cancelled appointments frequently. The AAMFT Ethics Committee received a complaint from a client who reported that the MFT had arrived "an hour late for the appointment, smelled of alcohol, and had slurred speech." The client transferred to another therapist for continued therapy.

COMMENTS: The MFT neglected to seek professional assistance and treatment that may have prevented the relapse and the impairment of work performance and clinical judgment, as well as preventing the violation of this subprinciple. It is crucial for a therapist who is suffering from loss, depression, substance abuse, or personal problems to contact a professional who can be objective and helpful in time of need. The therapist could have arranged for client coverage until recovery was achieved, and could have continued to receive supervision and guidance to assure ongoing recovery and professional competence and integrity.

3.4 Marriage and family therapists do not provide services that create a conflict of interest that may impair work performance or clinical judgment.

VIGNETTE: A therapist saw a 35-year old client for individual therapy whose primary complaint was that the spouse was unfaithful and violent toward the client. After six months, the spouse was asked to be included in marital therapy. The therapist agreed and continued to see the client for individual therapy too. The client later separated from the spouse and filed for divorce. The spouse complained to the AAMFT Ethics Committee that the therapist had shown favoritism and a bias toward the client during marital therapy and had not focused on the spouse's needs as also being significant and important.

COMMENTS: The therapist violated this principle by agreeing to see the client and spouse for marital therapy while simultaneously providing individual therapy to the client. This created a conflict of interest that may have impaired clinical judgment and objectivity. Seeing the client for both individual and marital therapy increased a risk of bias, especially in this case, in which safety and protection were primary issues because of domestic violence. It would have been appropriate to refer the couple to another professional for marital therapy, and to maintain individual therapy with the client to prevent bias and alignment with the client. The spouse could have also been referred for individual therapy to address the spouse's issues and needs.

3.5 Marriage and Family Therapists, as presenters, teachers, supervisors, consultants, and researchers, are dedicated to high standards of scholarship, present accurate information, and disclose potential conflicts of interest.

VIGNETTE: A pharmaceutical company employed a marriage and family therapist to present educational seminars on the effects of an individual's depression on the family system. As part of the contract, the MFT was asked to show videotapes of these seminars to clients who suffered from depression. However, the videotapes included an advertisement of an antidepressant medication the company promoted. The MFT did not perceive this as being a problem or a conflict of interest and continued to show the videotapes to these clients.

COMMENTS: The MFT violated this principle by agreeing to show the videotapes that advertised medication sold by the pharmaceutical company, because this created a conflict of interest and roles. As a presenter, the therapist can play an important and helpful role in imparting knowledge and education to clients and families affected by depression. However, by promoting the videotapes, the therapist can be perceived as endorsing not only the medication but the pharmaceutical company as well, and this would certainly contribute to a conflict of roles. This violation could have been avoided if the therapist had initially disclosed this conflict to the company and refused to enter into this agreement.

3.6 Marriage and Family Therapists maintain accurate and adequate clinical and financial records.

VIGNETTE: A client who changed MFTs after relocating to another state requested that the individual therapy records be sent from the previous therapist to the new therapist. While perusing the records, the new therapist noticed that the therapy notes were incomplete and unsigned, i.e., the type of therapy was not noted, therapy issues were very vague, progress was not described, and clear goals and objectives were not written. Even more blatant was the omission of an initial intake explaining why the client requested therapy. Thus, the new therapist made a complaint to the AAMFT Ethics Committee about the inadequacy of the records kept by the previous therapist.

COMMENTS: By keeping inadequate and incomplete records, the previous therapist exhibited incompetence and negligence and a willful violation of this ethical principle.

It is imperative when writing intake and therapy notes that clinical information be complete, clear, and concise, indicating the presenting problem, family history and dynamics, the client's progress, and specific goals and objectives. When transferring records to another professional, it is the MFT's responsibility to ascertain that the records are complete and correct to facilitate continuity of care and a smooth transition of services.

3.7 While developing new skills in specialty areas, Marriage and Family Therapists take steps to ensure the competence of their work, and protect clients from possible harm. Marriage and Family Therapists practice in specialty areas new to them only after appropriate education, training, or supervised experience.

VIGNETTE: An MFT whose specialty was working with learning disabled children accepted a referral to provide therapy to two racially mixed children from Guatemala who were adopted by a couple in North Carolina. The children spoke Spanish and were learning to speak English. They had been in the United States for eight months. The children exhibited defiant and rebellious behavior and difficulties in adapting to a new environment and culture. After three months of individual/family therapy, the adoptive parents complained to the therapist that the children's behavior was worsening and that their school grades were dropping. The MFT admitted to the parents a lack of sufficient experience in working with children who were experiencing adoption and cultural difficulties, as well as a lack of bilingual skills that made it difficult for the therapist to understand the children. The parents became angry with the MFT for accepting this referral and for contributing to the children's difficulties in adaptation and acclimation.

COMMENTS: It is imperative that therapists are cognizant of their professional limits and do not provide services in areas in which they lack education, training, or supervised experience. It is evident that this family would have benefited from receiving services from a therapist whose expertise was in the area of adoption and cultural issues in order to understand the significant stressors that children experience when adopted and relocated to an area that is culturally foreign to them. It would have been important to have a therapist who was bilingual, or have an interpreter who could have translated during the therapy process. In continuing therapy with this family without acquiring the necessary training and supervision or referring to an appropriate therapist, the MFT caused further stress and harm for the family.

3.8 Marriage and Family Therapists do not engage in sexual or other forms of harassment of clients, students, trainees, supervisees, employees, colleagues, or research subjects.

VIGNETTE: A client who was an incest survivor sought therapy from a church pastor who was also a marriage and family therapist. The therapist offered support and comforted the client with hugs and pats on the shoulder. Gradually, the touching increased to other parts of the body. The therapist made sexually inappropriate statements such as, "I dreamt that we were making love last night. Did you dream about me too?" The client developed significant guilt and shame and disclosed these incidents to a friend who reported the misconduct to the director of the church.

COMMENTS: The pastor/MFT engaged in harmful and damaging behavior toward the client through acts of sexual harassment and impropriety. Due to the power differential in the therapeutic relationship, the client was in a vulnerable position and in need of attention, validation, and comfort from the pastor. The sexual harassment may have triggered unresolved sexual issues for the client and contributed to feelings of guilt and shame. The therapist clearly took advantage of the client's vulnerability and manipulated the situation out of self-interest rather than placing the client's needs first. When a sexual attraction to a client occurs, it is the therapist's responsibility to immediately seek supervision in order to address and resolve this problem or to decide whether it is in the client's best interests to transfer to another therapist for continued therapy. It is important to note that this type of violation often results in the termination of membership as the AAMFT Ethics Committee does not tolerate sexual impropriety towards clients by members.

3.9 Marriage and Family Therapists do not engage in the exploitation of clients, trainees, supervisees, employees, colleague, or research subjects.

VIGNETTE: A graduate student in marriage and family therapy was awarded a teaching assistantship with a tenured and respected MFT professor. Assignments included teaching classes, grading tests and papers, and mentoring undergraduate students under the supervision of the professor. The student received credit hours for this work. As the semester progressed, the student began assuming more responsibility and work than was contracted for, and received less supervision and guidance from the professor. The student was fearful of confronting the professor and allowed this to continue for the remainder of the year. The student finally disclosed this problem to another professor who made a complaint to the head of the department.

COMMENTS: The MFT professor exploited the graduate student by allowing the student to assume more responsibility and work than was contracted for, which was compounded by the lack of necessary supervision and guidance required for the student's learning and training. This exploitation appeared self-serving on the professor's part and affected not only the graduate student, but also the undergraduate students who were dependent on the professor's guidance, judgment, and decision making. The professor also used position, authority, and power to manipulate and take advantage of the student whose performance appraisal was dependent on the professor's evaluation.

PRINCIPLE 3: SUBPRINCIPLES 3.10 THROUGH 3.15
PROFESSIONAL COMPETENCE AND INTEGRITY

Patrick O'Malley, Ph.D.

5

PRINCIPLE III PROFESSIONAL COMPETENCE AND INTEGRITY

Marriage and family therapists maintain high standards of professional competence and integrity.

3.10 Marriage and family therapists do not give to or receive from clients (a) gifts of substantial value or (b) gifts that impair the integrity or efficacy of the therapeutic relationship.

VIGNETTE (a): An MFT worked with a single parent for several months helping to deal with the terminal illness and death of the client's 13-year old child. As the months of grieving ensued, this parent stated several times that coming to therapy was the only time to feel safe expressing the deep pain of the loss. Because the clinician had visited the unit several times where the child was being treated, the client also felt that the therapist had formed a special bond with the child. The client presented a wrapped gift to the therapist on the year anniversary of the child's death. The gift was the child's favorite stuffed animal. The therapist was moved by this gesture and graciously accepted the gift.

COMMENTS (a): Setting a monetary limit to the gifts given to an MFT by a client may not sufficiently deal with the code statement "substantial value." In this case, if the MFT had set a $50 limit to any gift received from a client, the gift would have been acceptable. "Substantial value" must also mean substantial emotional or sentimental value. Clearly, this gift was significant in that way. To accept such a gift runs the risk of compromising the boundaries that are imperative to the integrity of the therapeutic relationship. A clinically appropriate explanation for declining the gift should be offered to the client.

VIGNETTE (b): A client was referred to an MFT after experiencing a devastating divorce. Early in the therapy the MFT discovered that the client had not experienced any independent activities during the marriage. The therapist suggested the therapeutic goal of creating some hobbies or activities in which the client could develop some individual identity. The client began collecting ceramic birds, reviving a hobby that had once been shared with an early romantic partner many years before, and the joy in this endeavor became part of the recovery process. The MFT spotted an unusual bird in an antique mall that cost only $10, and purchased the item, giving it to the client in the next session as reinforcement for the good work in therapy. Shortly before giving the gift, however, the therapist had begun to realize that the client had formed a significant transference, but the therapist gave the gift anyway because it was not an item of value. Indeed, the client's response to the gift seemed out of proportion to the intent in giving it. An effort to refer the case to another therapist was met with a complaint filed with the licensing board and AAMFT for abandonment of the therapy relationship. During the proceedings, the gift was used as evidence of the close relationship that had been formed.

COMMENTS (b): Once again, the financial value of the gift was not the issue. The MFT's self-perceived rationale for giving the gift seemed clinically appropriate, and the MFT was alert to the risk of giving gifts of significant financial value. But the MFT evidenced poor judgment by failing to weigh the client's history and likely perception of this act. There may also have been a failure to adequately monitor the MFT's own motivations for going through with giving the gift despite clear contraindications.

3.11 Marriage and family therapists do not diagnose, treat, or advise on problems outside the recognized boundaries of their competence.

VIGNETTE: A couple came to an MFT for marital therapy. The couple presented themselves as caught in a cycle of one partner expressing anger and the other withdrawing into a protective position. In one of the assessment sessions, the withdrawn partner complained of severe sleep depravation due to the depression experienced from the marriage. The partner stated resistance to any form of prescription medication. The therapist urged the partner try an herbal sleep remedy that some clients had recently reported as helpful, saying, "I'll bet that would take care of the problem." At this suggestion, the client tried the substance and ended up in the emergency room. The client's spouse lodged a complaint against the MFT for practicing medicine without a license.

COMMENTS: Marriage and family therapists should always exert special care when diagnosing, treating, or advising clients on related issues such as health. While marriage and family therapists may possess general knowledge in the areas of medicine, education, law, and other fields that impact the lives of clients, referrals should always be made when specific help is required. Because of clients' trust and dependency in treatment, therapists' comments and suggestions, even lightly made, may carry unintended weight.

When a client discusses options for addressing extra-therapeutic problems such as medical or legal difficulties, therapists must make it clear they are not providing directives, but are supporting the client in exploring those options and making their own decisions.

3.12 Marriage and family therapists make efforts to prevent the distortion or misuse of their clinical and research findings.

VIGNETTE: An MFT was noted for working with adults who experienced sexual abuse as a child. When a multiple victim case of sexual abuse involving a local minister came to the attention of the local press, this therapist was interviewed for an article. In the interview, the clinician stated that a statistically significant number of personally-treated cases had been victimized by clergy. The headline of the article read "Local Marriage and Family Therapist Says Most Sexual Abusers Are Clergy." The clinician did not take any action to correct this statement. The local ministers wrote several letters to the paper expressing outrage that a mental health professional would make such a statement.

COMMENTS: Marriage and family therapists should do everything possible to make sure the information given to any source is presented accurately. In this case the therapist should have insisted on previewing the material before it went to press. If a distortion is made public, the therapist should take every reasonable measure possible to correct the information.

3.13 Marriage and family therapists, because of their ability to influence and alter the lives of others, exercise special care when making public their professional recommendations and opinions through testimony or other public statements.

VIGNETTE: An MFT was subpoenaed to court to testify in a client's divorce case. This therapist had worked only with one of the spouses in the case. During the course of therapy, the client had described the spouse as an angry, self-centered person who had no regard for the rest of the family members. During one session the therapist suggested the client research Narcissistic Personality Disorder as a means of understanding the behavior of the other spouse. When testifying, the client's attorney made reference to the statement made in the session concerning this disorder. When questioned specifically, the therapist stated that given the information stated by the client, Narcissistic Personality Disorder was a reasonable diagnosis for the client's spouse. The client's spouse later filed a complaint with the licensing board and professional association stating that the testimony was damaging to the spouse's case.

COMMENTS: Marriage and family therapists must be cautious when making any statement that can be misunderstood or potentially used inappropriately. Even if the therapist had suggested the client read information about a disorder in order to better understand the client's spouse, the therapist should clearly state that a diagnosis is not being made on a person whom they have not treated. If the therapist had made this type of disclaimer in the session, the therapist could then clearly state the same in the courtroom.

3.14 To avoid a conflict of interests, marriage and family therapists who treat minors or adults involved in custody or visitation actions may not also perform forensic evaluations for custody, residence, or visitation of the minor. The marriage and family therapist who treats the minor may provide the court or mental health professional performing the evaluation with information about the minor from the marriage and family therapist's perspective as a treating marriage and family therapist, so long as the marriage and family therapist does not violate confidentiality.

VIGNETTE: An MFT saw a couple through several sessions in attempts to work out their long-standing marital conflict. The therapist also saw their three children separately at the request of both spouses to help the children deal with the conflict at home. When the couple decided to divorce, one of the spouses subpoenaed the therapy records for support in a custody suit. In the records were notes on the children's sessions in which all three children stated they would like to live with a specific parent, should their parents divorce. When called to testify, the therapist was asked if the children's preference for the parent with whom they wished to live was the choice the MFT would support for the more adequate and competent parent. The therapist stated agreement with the children's position given the clinical experience in working with the parents. The parent who lost the custody suit later sued the MFT.

COMMENTS: This new section of the Code of Ethics gives marriage and family therapists a solid position from which to refuse to render opinions when involved in custody and visitation disputes. Unless the therapist's only role with the family has been the performance of a forensic evaluation using the standard of care protocols commonly used in the community, a marriage and family therapist should only reveal information gained in the role of a treating therapist and not as an evaluator. The therapist in the vignette essentially accepted an invitation to render an expert opinion as to the preferable parent without performing the necessary examination as an independent evaluator. The therapist should have stood firm in declining to give an opinion regarding the more competent parent. Historically, taking such a position was difficult when attorneys and judges insisted on an answer. Marriage and family therapists can now state that giving such an opinion would be a violation of the ethical code. The MFT in the vignette may have also violated confidentiality if both parents did not sign a waiver to release confidential information (Subprinciple 2.2).

3.15 Marriage and family therapists are in violation of this Code and subject to termination of membership or other appropriate action if they: (a) are convicted of any felony; (b) are convicted of a misdemeanor related to their qualifications or functions; (c) engage in conduct which could lead to a conviction of a felony, or a misdemeanor related to their qualifications or functions; (d) are expelled from or disciplined by other professional organizations; (e) have their licenses or certificates suspended or revoked or are otherwise disciplined by regulatory bodies; (f) continue to practice marriage and family therapy while no longer competent to do so because they are impaired by physical or mental causes or the abuse of alcohol or other substances; or (g) fail to cooperate with the Association at any point from the inception of an ethical complaint through the completion of all proceedings regarding that complaint.

VIGNETTE (a): An MFT attracted a number of business owners as clients by giving talks to civic and business groups on the dynamics of family businesses. In session, clients often shared privileged information regarding the status of their business deals. The clinician bought stock in a business prior to an acquisition that significantly increased the value of the stock. One client was later charged and convicted of insider trading. A list was given to the authorities of all persons who had knowledge of the acquisition. The therapist was listed and subsequently received a felony conviction.

COMMENTS (a): The MFT violated the code the moment the purchase of stock was made. Any felony conviction is considered a violation of the code even if it is not directly related to client care. Members who do not uphold the law reflect poorly on the field and harm the reputation of the profession.

VIGNETTE (b): An MFT was subpoenaed to appear in court and to be prepared to testify and provide treatment records in a custody suit. In a meeting in the judge's chambers to inspect the records for relevance to the suit, the therapist stated that all records on the case were on a computer program that crashed, and consequently the records were unavailable. The judge ruled that this failure to maintain any clinical records was a violation of the record-keeping requirement under the licensure law, and also constituted contempt of court. The MFT was found guilty of contempt, which is a misdemeanor and was fined $1,000.

COMMENTS (b): This conviction was related to the marriage and family therapist's professional behavior. This section of the code communicates the need for MFTs to understand the laws related to professional standards of care and to comply with these laws to the highest standard of professional behavior.

VIGNETTE (c): An MFT consulted as a supervisor in a group home for children and adolescents. During a group supervision session, a counselor confessed to becoming physically violent with a resident during the previous evening shift. The supervisor processed the conflict with the counselor and the team. The counselor was better able to understand what triggered the reaction to the resident. The resident, however, managed to call Child Protective Services and an investigation began that included the supervising MFT who failed to report the incident. Another counselor on the team filed a complaint against the MFT.

COMMENTS (c): While not yet proven guilty, the MFT engaged in conduct as a professional therapist that could lead to a conviction by not reporting the confessed abuse to the proper authorities. Marriage and family therapists must be aware of the behaviors that are necessary to comply with state law and standards of care.

VIGNETTE (d, e): A licensing board charged an MFT with committing serious billing fraud. The charges were substantiated and consequently the therapist lost licensure as a psychologist and as a member in several professional associations. The licensing board reported the action to the AAMFT Ethics Committee and consequently the member was charged with violations of subprinciples 3.15 (d) and (e), as well as subprinciple 7.4 for the underlying misconduct. After hearing the member's defense, the Committee found the member in violation on all charges.

COMMENTS (d, e): AAMFT shares and receives information on a national level with other professional associations and licensing boards. The Ethics Committee gives the findings of other disciplinary bodies a presumption of validity and appropriateness unless the charged member can show this presumption is unwarranted. Specifically, the member may be able to demonstrate that the other body failed to provide adequate due process, or that the other body's sanction was excessively severe.

VIGNETTE (f): An MFT returned to work one week after a spouse's death. While the MFT's clients were compassionate about the difficult loss, several dropped out of therapy and complained to their new therapists that the mourning therapist was often tearful and distracted. Several of the MFT's colleagues tried to discuss their concern directly, but the grieving therapist insisted there was no problem. One of the clients subsequently filed a complaint with the Ethics Committee stating that the MFT was more concerned with talking about the loss than with the client's needs.

COMMENTS (f): Marriage and family therapists are not immune from the same experiences that impact clients. Alcohol or substance abuse, grief, depression, and physical illness are some of the ways that therapists may become impaired and unable to properly care for clients' needs. MFT's must be able to recognize when personal issues affect the ability to perform professional duties. Colleagues need to keep a watchful eye on peers who are reported to be acting incompetently, and they need to intervene appropriately.

VIGNETTE (g): An MFT was reported to the Ethics Committee for an improper dual relationship with a client. This therapist was a long-standing member of the Association and had held several local and national offices. Upon receiving the charge letter from the Ethics Committee, the therapist wrote back that the charge was an insult to an exemplary professional reputation, and that no response would be forthcoming. The therapist was exhorted to comply with the investigation, but sent no further correspondence.

COMMENTS (g): Marriage and family therapists are required to cooperate with Ethics Committee investigations regarding their professional conduct. Due process must be served for the AAMFT Code of Ethics to serve the public good. A charge of a potential violation of the AAMFT Code of Ethics does not constitute a violation unless and until the preponderance of evidence in the case supports the charges. In rare cases, when the evidence is overwhelming in its clarity and reliability, the Committee has the power to find a violation even without hearing a defense from the charged member. The Committee strongly prefers that every ethics case investigation include receipt of a full defense from the member including all material the member deems relevant. MFTs who believe themselves innocent of potential violations of the AAMFT Code of Ethics are obligated to do their part to help the Committee determine whether or not the Code was in fact violated. Members who decline to cooperate with the Committee's truth-finding mission are reneging on an important duty to the profession and, even if "innocent" of the original charges, are unfortunately sure to be found in violation of subprinciple 3.15 (g).

Principle Four: Responsibility to Students and Supervisees

Maria T. Flores, Ph.D.

6

Principle IV Marriage and family therapists do not exploit the trust and dependency of students and supervisees.

A marriage and family therapist's responsibility to students and supervisees is a serious, multileveled, and important responsibility. Inherent in these relationships are very positive dual or multiple relationships. Some multiple relationships, however, can exploit the trust and dependency of students and supervisees. There is the responsibility of teaching and training a future marriage and family therapist and also the sense that these students and supervisees will be one's future colleagues. This position of viewing students and supervisees as future colleagues, and therefore, equals, is a collaborative stance. It is a stance to be encouraged rather than avoided.

4.1 Marriage and family therapists are aware of their influential positions with respect to students and supervisees, and they avoid exploiting the trust and dependency of such persons. Therapists, therefore, make every effort to avoid conditions and multiple relationships that could impair professional objectivity or increase the risk of exploitation. When the risk of impairment or exploitation exists due to conditions or multiple roles, therapists take appropriate precautions.

VIGNETTE: A professor was a real family person, with three children and a wonderful spouse. The professor's spouse was a lawyer with an outstanding reputation in the city. As a university faculty member, the professor had a more flexible work schedule than an attorney's, and the professor often took the kids to the university. All the students really enjoyed having the children around as they were well behaved. Once there was an emergency in the clinic and one of the students took care of the children. After a time, however, the professor began asking stu dents to baby-sit when the couple needed a night out. Or sometimes, students would be asked to watch the kids while the professor was teaching a class or attending a meeting. This situation seemed innocent enough but the word spread and students felt that they could not say no without jeopardizing their relationship with the professor.

COMMENTS: Many dual or multiple relationship conflicts, such as the above baby-sitting case, are handled in the department or in the clinic and never reported to the AAMFT Ethics Committee. For example, it is common practice for supervisors to switch supervisees if a mutual romantic attraction is acknowledged. Or the professor/supervisor may choose to switch the student to simply avoid a situation of intense interaction with that student when such an attraction on the part of either party is realized. Students and supervisees may request to be transferred if the relational fit is extremely uncomfortable. Multiple relationship conflicts occur and efforts to avoid exploitation in those situations are imperative. It is essential for professors and supervisors to wonder, "Can a student say *no* to this seemingly innocent request?" That is, say no without fear of negative consequences?

In time, a student or supervisee may be a fellow faculty member, committee member, coworker or coauthor. A reversal of roles could even occur so one's student or supervisee ends up as a future employer or department chair! Even more complicated is the fact that students, supervisees, faculty members, and supervisors intermingle during training programs, often sharing meals together, going to joint parties or social affairs, meeting at conferences, planning workshops, and collaborating in areas of interest. Faculty and supervisors, therefore, need to take appropriate precautions to avoid impairing objectivity and risking exploitation of their students and supervisees. When making a request of one's trainee, the major question of concern should be, "Is this request beneficial for the student/supervisee's professional growth?"

It is important for the faculty members and supervisors to understand their authority and influence, even if it only exists temporarily as students and supervisees move more and more into a peer relationship.

An understanding of the power differential and the possibility for exploitation needs to be acknowledged at all times but especially when the age distribution is close and a student or supervisee is gifted with many talents. Consideration of the dynamics of transference and counter-transference may be appropriate. Sometimes the power differential is difficult to sense. The power differential is clearly defined however, when the faculty member or supervisor assesses skills and abilities, and must grade performance. Paid positions or assistantships for which students compete, and for which faculty members have influence, could also be used as venues for exploitation. Because the relationship between supervisor or faculty member and the trainee is for some time an unequivocally hierarchical relationship, the possibility of exploitation exists. At all times, it is the responsibility of the supervisor or faculty member to ensure that exploitation never occurs.

4.2 Marriage and family therapist do not provide therapy to current students or supervisees.

VIGNETTE: Students and supervisees meet with crises during their training and it is natural to turn to their professor or supervisor. On one occasion, a supervisee's brother committed suicide and the supervisee went to the supervisor in tears. The supervisor listened as a professional friend and consultant, but then referred the supervisee to a psychotherapist. This supervisee remained in supervision with the supervisor and used the experience to help others in the consultation group when case examples of suicidal ideation arose.

COMMENTS: In this example, the supervisor assessed the supervisee's crisis and referred when psychotherapy was deemed necessary. A supervisor who attempted to act as therapist would compromise the supervisory relationship. The ability to act as an objective evaluator of the trainee's performance would be compromised. Marriage and family therapists do not provide therapy to current students or supervisees, because of the freedom of interaction and natural multiple relationships between faculty and students and supervisor and supervisees. Providing therapy to students would blur the boundaries helpful in an educational environment.

A therapist is responsible for the emotional and mental well being of the patient or clients in care. Clients have vulnerability with a psychotherapist that helps the therapeutic process. Vulnerability is meaningful in the therapeutic process, but this type of responsibility or therapeutic care is not applicable to a student–teacher role or a supervisee–supervisor relationship. This type of vulnerability is not required, encouraged, or needed between supervisor and supervisees or between faculty and student for the process of education. Harm could occur to the supervisee if the person who was known as their empathic, nonjudgmental therapist had to criticize the supervisee's clinical expertise or schoolwork. Supervisees may not do the required training or be lax in their efforts if they believe that their therapist/supervisor will "give them a good grade" because they have such a close relationship. The structure of the educational system and the very nature of the supervisors and supervisees would dramatically have to change, because greater boundaries are required between therapist and client. However, being compassionate with students when a student is in crisis is encouraged.

VIGNETTE: Another supervisee was accused of sexual harassment of a patient. This supervisee also turned to the supervisor for therapeutic help. Again, the supervisor consulted with the supervisee on the issues and referred the supervisee to a psychotherapist and a lawyer. This supervisee discontinued supervision and only returned when all charges were dropped.

COMMENTS: Sometimes a change of supervision group or professor is necessary when a crisis occurs. In this case, supervision did not continue. While the case was in the courts, a separation was necessary to avoid the supervisee disclosing confidential information to other members of the supervision group. This also protected the supervisor and supervisee from being subpoenaed to testify on a matter unknown to them.

4.3 Marriage and family therapists do not engage in sexual intimacy with students or supervisees during the evaluative or training relationship between the therapist and student or supervisee. Should a supervisor engage in sexual activity with a former supervisee, the burden of proof shifts to the supervisor to demonstrate that there has been no exploitation or injury to the supervisee.

VIGNETTE: At a university, one student was suspected by other students of having a relationship with a professor. The gossip was at a high pitch when this student was awarded a research assistantship. Students grumbled that this student was not the most qualified. The professor making the final decision was the person accused of being biased because of an affair. Later, the same student was awarded another paid assistantship at the university. No student had previously received both assistantships prior to that year. Again some students made accusations of an affair as they stated that this faculty member and the student spent many hours behind closed doors at the clinic and at the university offices. Other students also accused bias in the classroom and in the clinic. Both the professor and the student denied all accusations to others, though no formal charges were made.

It was only when the "breakup" occurred that more substantial information came to light. The student told another student, and a formal complaint was made to the faculty grievance committee. Other students came forward with accusations of sexual harassment. After two years of meetings and appeals, the university took away the professor's job, and professional licenses and memberships were lost. These events shattered the professor's life and created great pain for the professor's spouse and children.

COMMENTS: Both parties lost. One was clearly exploited. Professors and supervisors hold power over their students and supervisees. Sexual liaisons cannot be simple mutual consenting relationships under these conditions. The possibility of harm occurring in the wake of the affair is likely and the damages are great. Not only was the student harmed in this vignette, but also fellow students were given unfair treatment in their education. The professor, too, needed help, but was ruined before addressing the underlying relational problems. The pain and suffering incurred by the professor's family was also a heavy price of the clandestine affair. Even if there had never been a sexual affair, the appearance of one, and the ongoing special treatment of one student should have been addressed and corrected by the professor before the situation was out of control.

Vignette: A former student, 25 years old, saw a 30-year old professor at a class reunion party. They had a long discussion and found that they were both originally from Wyoming. Both knew similar vacations spots, and they discovered that they were probably at the same campsite when they were teenagers. They had a great laugh about this and decided to go out to dinner. After dating for about a year, they decided to marry. They had a wonderful wedding with both former students and faculty attending.

COMMENTS: This is an example of a rare case when the result is satisfactory to both parties. These situations do happen. One factor that made a difference in this case was the age of the two parties. Because their ages were close, the student did not have the same awe toward the professor that might have been the case if the professor had been an older and more established professional. The student had been in one of the professor's classes, and had experienced good teaching undistorted by any hidden or dual agenda. The professor was always appropriate with students and supervisees. Additionally, the professor's evaluative authority over the student had ended with the class years ago, so no continuing relationship around recommendation letters was an issue. Had the prior hierarchical relationship been that of supervisor–supervisee, the professor would be held to a higher standard concerning the sexual relationship. In part, this is because the supervisory relationship creates a lingering power differential due to its greater psychological intimacy and the continuing need for the supervisor to serve as a reference and advocate.

4.4 Marriage and family therapists do not permit students or supervisees to perform or hold themselves out as competent to perform professional services beyond their training level of experience and competence.

VIGNETTE: A student was completing the requirements toward graduating with a Ph.D. in Marriage and Family Therapy. The student had most of the dissertation completed and therefore assumed that putting "Ph.D." on a business card was acceptable. The student showed the card to the dissertation committee chair, who neglected to say that these cards could not be used until after the doctorate had been officially awarded. A client reported the situation to the university, the licensing board, and to AAMFT for misrepresentation of professional credentials.

COMMENTS: Unfortunately, the student's career began with letters from AAMFT and the licensing board demanding to "cease and desist practicing at a level beyond your training and experience." The professor and the department head also received a letter from AAMFT reminding the department of subprinciple 4.4 and its implications for students. Although only two months away from graduation, the misrepresentation was still wrong because the student had not, in fact, completed earning a doctorate. The client who filed the complaints was offended that the student claimed to be a Ph.D. and did not yet hold that degree. The client's level of trust in therapy was harmed by the misrepresentation. Having told one lie, were there others? Although the student personally bore most of the responsibility for this ethical lapse, the committee chair missed an easy opportunity to take corrective action.

4.5 Marriage and family therapists take reasonable measures to ensure that services provided by the supervisee are professional.

VIGNETTE: A therapist, who was clearly competent and had a great rapport with clients, was receiving referrals from former clients, which is unusual in a university setting with beginning clinicians. Wanting to try hypnosis with clients requesting this type of work, the therapist asked a supervisor for supervision in this area. The supervisor agreed, but was not trained in this area. The work began. One client was unsettled by the hypnosis experience and sued the therapist, the supervisor, and the outpatient clinic where the therapy work was being conducted. The out of court settlement found the supervisor guilty of misrepresenting credentials as a supervisor in an area without training. A hefty financial settlement was sanctioned. The therapist in training received a minor fine and was encouraged to check the credential of supervisors before contracting them for training. The outpatient clinic was cleared of misrepresentation. However, all incurred financial payments to the lawyers.

COMMENTS: Supervisors must not assume they are skilled in specialized areas without formal training. The supervisor must always put the welfare of the client before the teaching of the therapist. Supervisees have a responsibility to be conscientious consumers of supervision services.

4.6 Marriage and family therapists avoid accepting as supervisees or students those individuals with whom a prior or existing relationship could compromise the therapist's objectivity. When such situations cannot be avoided, therapists take appropriate precautions to maintain objectivity. Examples of such relationships include, but are not limited to, those individuals with whom the therapist has a current or prior sexual, close personal, immediate familial, or therapeutic relationship.

VIGNETTE: Jamie, an AAMFT Approved Supervisor, is one of two clinical supervisors at a small training program far from any other training programs. Gray, a student who recently transferred into the program happens to be married to one of Jamie's younger siblings. Because this familial relationship could compromise Jamie's supervisory judgment through favoritism or for other reasons, it has been agreed that the student will receive clinical supervision from the program's other supervisor. However, that supervisor unexpectedly departed from the program, leaving the student without supervision. It was unknown how long it would be before a replacement was found. In the meantime Jamie had to take over all supervisory duties, as no other qualified individual was available.

Jamie initiated precautions to ensure an appropriate supervisory relationship with Gray during this interim period. First Jamie candidly discussed the situation with the head of the program: Jamie's personal history with Gray was not exceptionally close but had been favorable and untroubled. Gray had demonstrated an ability to differentiate clearly between roles. Also, Gray had been doing well in the program and had established good relationships. Given these factors, it appeared the major risk was the appearance of favoritism. Consequently, the situation was explained to all the other supervisees so it was out in the open. The program head met with the supervision group and encouraged anyone who perceived favoritism or other undesirable consequences to raise the issue in whatever way was most comfortable: in the group itself, with Jamie privately, or with the program head privately. The program head was at least initially present during Jamie's individual supervisory sessions with Gray, to reinforce the professional relationship and monitor for appropriateness. It was agreed that Jamie would not write any letters of reference for Gray. Rather, the new supervisor who was to be hired as soon as possible would do this. Other steps would be developed as needed.

COMMENTS: This vignette illustrates not a violation but "appropriate precautions" when a potentially problematic multiple relationship with a supervisee is unavoidable. Subprinciple 4.6 recognizes that in the real world such relationships cannot always be neatly avoided. Sometimes a creative solution is required if everyone is to benefit. Consultation with trusted and competent third parties is essential to assess risks and develop a workable solution. Bringing the issue into the open with affected parties such as the other supervisees is important for maintaining trust. These parties must have avenues for addressing grievances or concerns. The situation here would not be acceptable for the long term. Because of the precautions taken it is acceptable as a short-term solution to the program's crisis.

4.7 Marriage and family therapists do not disclose supervisee confidences except by written authorization or waiver, or when mandated or permitted by law. In educational or training settings where there are multiple supervisors, disclosures are permitted only to other professional colleagues, administrators, or employers who share responsibility for training of the supervisee. Verbal authorization will not be sufficient except in emergency situations, unless prohibited by law.

VIGNETTE: A student, who was at the top of the class, was well liked and had the prospect of a great professional future. In the last semester of training, the student was diagnosed with cancer. It spread rapidly. The student was unable to complete the program and died in the fall of the next year. The student had often told family members how wonderful one professor was, offering support throughout the student's struggles and throughout the entire ordeal. The family's offer for this professor to say a few words at the funeral service was accepted.

The professor spoke of personal information shared in supervision class when the group was discussing drugs and alcohol abuse. The information was common knowledge to many students because the personal discussion was carried over into lunch on more than one occasion. And though it was common knowledge to the student's immediate family, it was unknown to friends, extended family, other students, and faculty attending the service. The family was outraged by the comments. They expected a sound affirmation of the student's worth as a student, as a young therapist, and as a person in relationship, but never a disclosure of past problems. The family reported the professor's conduct to the university, to the AAMFT Ethics Committee, and to the licensing board.

COMMENTS: Confidentiality is a serious concern for professors and supervisors. Disclosing information learned in supervision about a supervisee is not acceptable, even after the supervisee's death. The professor was misguided in thinking that because the student continued conversations of a personal nature outside of supervision in such an open way, this information was not confidential. Sorting through what was said in supervision and out of the supervisions context is much too complicated to discern. Confidentiality is the responsibility of the supervisor, not the supervisee, in a one to one situation. In a group of supervisees, the supervisor and the supervisees are bound to uphold confidentiality concerning other supervisees' sharing.

PRINCIPLE 5: RESPONSIBILITY TO RESEARCH PARTICIPANTS

7

Eric E. McCollum, Ph.D., and Lisa D. Locke, M.S.

Eric E. McCollum, Ph.D., and Lisa D. Locke, M.S.

PRINCIPLE V RESPONSIBILITY TO RESEARCH PARTICIPANTS

Investigators respect the dignity and protect the welfare of research participants, and are aware of applicable laws and regulations and professional standards governing the conduct of research.

5.1 Investigators are responsible for making careful examinations of ethical acceptability in planning studies. To the extent that services to research participants may be compromised by participation in research, investigators seek the ethical advice of qualified professionals not directly involved in the investigation and observe safeguards to protect the rights of research participants.

VIGNETTE: A researcher developed an 18-week "therapy only" group treatment model for depression and was conducting a study of its effectiveness. Participants volunteered to be a part of the study and were screened out if they were currently in treatment or taking medication for depression. The researcher planned to take data at the beginning, middle, and end of treatment, as well as three months following treatment. During the midway data point at the ninth week, participants filled out a qualitative and quantitative self-report survey. In the evaluation, one participant reported that the group had been extremely helpful. That participant noted benefits from working with other clients who shared the same struggles, a decrease in depressive symptoms, and a significant reduction in depression compared to pre-test. The participant also indicated on the self-report that antidepressant medication had been initiated six weeks ago due to suicidal ideation. The researcher was entering the data from the self-report survey and came upon that participant's responses. The participant was immediately called and asked not to return to the group.

COMMENTS: The researcher failed to consult with a colleague who was not directly involved with the study. While the study was testing the effectiveness of a "therapy only" group treatment model, the participant in question clearly indicated benefiting from the group, even though the participant was also taking antidepressant medication. Through a discussion with a professional not directly involved in the project, the researcher could have examined alternatives and possibly come to a resolution that wouldn't have compromised the participant's treatment or the study. One possibility would have been to have the participant continue in the group, but exclude the associated data from the research study. Another would have been to find alternative treatment for that participant. The researcher was blinded by a quest to prove the model effective. When designing a research study, the best interests of the client should supersede the research.

5. 2 Investigators requesting participant involvement in research inform participants of the aspects of the research that might reasonably be expected to influence willingness to participate. Investigators are especially sensitive to the possibility of diminished consent when participants are also receiving clinical services, or have impairments which limit understanding and/or communication, or when participants are children.

VIGNETTE: An MFT worked at an agency and had been facilitating a group for Adult Children of Alcoholics. The group met for seven weeks. To help secure funding for the agency for the upcoming year, the therapist decided to include data from the group in an ongoing research project that the agency was running. The group was informed of the decision at the beginning of the next session and was asked to sign an informed consent agreement. In this agreement, the group members were informed of their rights as participants in the research study and that the sessions would be videotaped. They were informed that after each session they would fill out an evaluation that would not be seen by the facilitator, and that they could skip any question they preferred not to answer. They were also informed that they had the right to withdraw from the project at any time and would be given referrals for other treatment options. The therapist gave the group information about the project and, before anyone was given the informed consent agreement, the therapist noted that if anyone did not want to participate in the research to begin with, there was a list of referrals where those individuals could continue their treatment. The list included a new group being formed within the agency, facilitated by another therapist that would not be part of the research project. Everyone in the group signed the consent form and the group proceeded.

COMMENTS: The intent of the research study was not inimical to, and was arguably of potential benefit to, the future well being of the clients. Yet, the therapist did not take into account the principle of diminished consent upon asking the therapy group to participate. The group had already formed and had received seven weeks of treatment. Since the group members had probably already bonded and established a therapeutic relationship with the facilitator, having their therapist ask the group members if they wanted to participate may have influenced the clients' willingness to participate, especially since they would have to leave the group if they chose not to participate. Even though careful steps were taken to provide referrals for other treatment options, including another group within the agency, the therapist violated Subprinciple 5.2.

5.3 Investigators respect each participant's freedom to decline participation in or to withdraw from a research study at any time. This obligation requires special thought and consideration when investigators or other members of the research team are in positions of authority or influence over participants. Marriage and family therapists, therefore, make every effort to avoid multiple relationships with research participants that could impair professional judgment or increase the risk of exploitation.

VIGNETTE: A professor was conducting research about how a history of physical abuse in childhood may influence parenting style. The professor asked parents whose children came to the university's daycare center if they would be willing to participate in the study. Those who agreed to participate signed an informed consent form assuring them, among other things, that they were free to withdraw from the study at any time, and that they could decline to answer any questions asked them during the research interview. One parent, who initially agreed to participate, became tearful when the interviewer began to ask about experiences of physical abuse in childhood, and said that the interview was too stressful to continue. The interviewer immediately suspended all questioning and suggested that the parent seek counseling at the campus MFT clinic if such counseling was desired. Later, the interviewer reviewed the interview process with the professor and the other project staff at a regular project staff meeting to make sure that research protocol had been followed correctly. It happened that the parent was also a student in the professor's graduate seminar that semester. The professor spoke to the parent after the next class, stating concern and again encouraging use of the clinic's services. At the end of the semester, the parent received a C- in the seminar. Angry about the situation, the parent told the professor that the low grade was obviously in retaliation for dropping out of the research project and that a grievance would be filed with the university's Human Subjects Committee and with the AAMFT Ethics Committee.

COMMENTS: In this case, the professor and the project interviewer did a number of things right. The parent's right to withdraw from the study was made clear in the consent process and the interviewer responded appropriately by suspending questions immediately when asked to. The interviewer suggested a resource that could be used if distress from the interview continued. Finally, the professor provided regular supervision and oversight to the interviewers working in the project to ensure that they followed the research protocol and complied with human subjects requirements.

Despite the care the professor had taken, the mere existence of a dual relationship left the door open to charges of misconduct. In this case, the best protection would have been barring any of the professor's students from participating in this research project, thereby avoiding a dual relationship. In other cases, the researcher might have been able to collect data anonymously, or to have a co-investigator deal with any research participants where there was the potential of a dual relationship. In this case, however, the professor was the only person in charge of the project and needed to carefully supervise the collection of data since the interviews dealt with a potentially upsetting subject area.

5.4 Information obtained about a research participant during the course of an investigation is confidential unless there is a waiver previously obtained in writing. When the possibility exists that others, including family members, may obtain access to such information, this possibility, together with the plan for protecting confidentiality, is explained as part of the procedure for obtaining informed consent.

VIGNETTE: The MFT clinic at a university was conducting a study about children and parents' views of therapy. Researchers interviewed parents and children separately following a therapy session. One couple, Kim and Robin, agreed to participate in the study and gave permission for Reed, their 9-year old child, to be interviewed. The informed consent form said that all information given to the researcher would be treated as confidential. When interviewed, Reed described a dislike for therapy and a feeling of no support from the family's therapist. While doodling on a piece of paper, Reed seemed to have difficulty and switched hands several times. When asked why, Reed muttered, "I have to write with my wrong arm because Kim yanks me around a lot when I'm bad. This last time I thought my whole arm was gonna come off." Reed voluntarily showed the interviewer bruises, allegedly from two nights ago. Immediately after this interview, the interviewer told the therapist and the clinical supervisor what Reed had said. The therapist asked Kim and Robin to come back into a therapy room and explained that, with the information that had emerged, a report to Child Protective Services must be made. Kim became irate, saying that the researcher had no right to share what Reed had said with the therapist, that it was a lie, and that Reed's bruises came from a bicycle accident. "And what's more," said Kim, "I would never have let you talk to my child if I'd known you were going to use the information against me."

COMMENTS: In this case, the interviewer violated Subprinciple 5.4 by failing to obtain a written waiver from the client—in this case one of the parents since Reed was a minor—before sharing any information gathered as part of the research project with the family's therapist. Because the research project was being conducted in the MFT clinic, the temptation to blur boundaries was great, but doing so did not meet the standard of ethical practice in this case. A further concern is that it was not made clear to the family that the researcher had a statutory duty to report cases of suspected child abuse. This should have been done as part of getting consent from the family for their participation in the research project. In any case, without a written release, the researcher's only obligation was to report Reed's allegations to Child Protective Services, and not to the therapist or supervisor.

Principle 6:
Responsibility to the Profession

Samuel T. Gladding, Ph.D.

8

Principle **VI** Responsibility to the Profession

Marriage and family therapists respect the rights and responsibilities of professional colleagues and participate in activities that advance the goals of the profession.

6.1 Marriage and family therapists remain accountable to the standards of the profession when acting as members or employees of organizations. If the mandates of an organization with which a marriage and family therapist is affiliated, through employment, contract or otherwise, conflict with the AAMFT Code of Ethics, marriage and family therapists make known to the organization their commitment to the AAMFT Code of Ethics and attempt to resolve the conflict in a way that allows the fullest adherence to the Code of Ethics.

VIGNETTE: A therapist is on a provider panel with a managed care organization (MCO). When the time comes to renew the contract, the therapist notices that an ominous new clause has been added: in order to improve its quality assurance functions, the MCO is claiming the right to inspect the clinical records of ALL the therapist's clients, whether or not each client is one of the MCO's customers. The therapist is uncomfortable with this arrangement, but figures it is unlikely the company will exercise this power. The therapist thinks of the numerous odious clauses embedded in apartment leases, car rentals, and even things like a whitewater rafting company's waiver of liability which seem unreasonable but which are never enforced. Thus, the therapist sighs, thinks, "what can you do?" and signs the MCO's contract.

A short time later the therapist's stomach flips upon receiving a phone call—an MCO representative is coming to do a random inspection of clinical files "as you agreed in your contract with us." Too late, the therapist mounts a counterattack to defend the confidentiality rights of those clients who are not customers of the MCO. Despite assistance from an attorney, the therapist's position is greatly weakened by the contract that had been signed without contesting the objectionable clause.

COMMENTS: In this case the therapist is right in trying to mount a counterattack to defend the confidentiality rights of those clients who are not customers of the MCO. After all, confidentiality is the bedrock on which therapeutic trust is built and as such there are huge ethical consequences to it being broken.

Unfortunately, what the therapist is trying to do may be futile. Since the therapist signed the contract with the MCO without protest, knowing full well that the odious clause was there, the therapist has little room to maneuver. Legally, the therapist has almost no recourse. Ethically, the therapist is in the same bind. A possible positive action the therapist could take is to appeal to the MCO representative's own sense of ethics, emphasizing the universal principles of beneficence, nonmaleficence, and fidelity that underlie ethical decision making while explaining how an inspection of all records would be ethically damaging. The therapist's commitment to the AAMFT Code of Ethics should also be disclosed to the representative and the thought process the therapist used should be explained as well. By doing so, the therapist might persuade the inspector to review only those cases covered by the MCO and not others. However, even if the outcome is not altered and the representative insists that all cases be open, the therapist will have tried to rectify the situation in the best possible way.

Another scenario in this situation, if the inspector insists on reviewing all cases, is for the therapist to protest the action in writing and make it known that signing another contract like the one signed in this case will be out of the question in the future. This type of move is one that focuses on exerting as much power as the therapist can muster instead of verbally appealing to principles, explanations, and persuasion. The climate, if these tactics are used, becomes adversarial and tense but there is a chance that the outcome may change.

A final dramatic action the therapist could consider regarding the inspection would be to resign and seek other employment. However it would be very difficult to do so without abandoning clients and disrupting treatment. This last option might not benefit anyone in the long run and so it should be weighed most carefully before it is executed. Clearly though, the therapist cannot continue to work in an environment where ethical standards are compromised.

Regardless of the tactics used or the outcome, the clinician should make the circumstances of this case known through professional publications and presentations, such as MFT newsletters, journals, or workshops. If the clinician does so, other practitioners may profit from the mistake and not find themselves stuck in similar situations. It is always better to object to an ethically questionable policy prior to its implementation than to try to fight it after it has been put in place. Never sign a document that has the potential to compromise professional standards no matter how benign it seems at the time.

6.2 Marriage and family therapists assign publication credit to those who have contributed to a publication in proportion to their contributions and in accordance with customary professional publication practices.

VIGNETTE: A professor decided to do a massive study on couple communication and placed an advertisement in a local paper for volunteers. At the same time, the professor enlisted a graduate student to help conduct the research. All went well in gathering data. However, in writing the report, the professor made a couple of serious statistical errors that, left uncorrected, would have made the report's conclusions incorrect. Fortunately, the graduate student caught the mistakes, told the professor, and then made the necessary corrections. When the study was published the professor took sole credit for the project without ever mentioning the assistance received from the graduate student.

COMMENTS: The professor made an error in judgment and ethics in handling this research matter. Although it is not unusual for professors to hire graduate students to help them collect data, it is wrong to not acknowledge their contributions to a project of this caliber, at least in a footnote, especially if the contribution was significant. The professor's failure to mention the graduate student's contribution to the study in this case was especially egregious. Had the graduate student not discovered the statistical mistakes, the paper that grew out of the research would have contained incorrect data and conclusions if it been published, and it may not have been published at all because of its questionable results. Thus, a footnote thanking the graduate student would have been in order and the professor might even have considered making the student a coauthor.

In writing a publication, it is better to err on the side of being inclusive than being exclusive. Few authors or researchers work alone. Acknowledging a person or persons for contributing to a final paper does not detract from the writer's initiative, effort, and results. A failure to do so does detract from the writer's integrity.

6.3 Marriage and family therapists do not accept or require authorship credit for a publication based on research from a student's program, unless the therapist made a substantial contribution beyond being a faculty advisor or research committee member. Coauthorship on a student thesis, dissertation, or project should be determined in accordance with principles of fairness and justice.

VIGNETTE: A graduate student was in the last year of an MFT program and needed a new dissertation advisor because the previously assigned advisor had moved. The student approached a professor who was in the process of applying for tenure. The professor agreed to chair the committee and be the faculty advisor, but in return, the professor had the student agree to assist in producing a publishable manuscript from the dissertation.

The professor was very demanding and made the graduate student revise the dissertation many times. When the dissertation was finished, however, it was exemplary, and the student received accolades from fellow students and the faculty. Shortly after the defense, the professor presented the student with a shortened manuscript of the dissertation and proposed to send out the manuscript to a prestigious periodical to be considered for publication. The professor's name appeared as the lead author; the student's was listed second. The professor explained to the student that the first author of a publication was the one who had done the most work on the manuscript, and that because of the extraordinary amount of time the professor had spent helping the student, the professor's name should be listed first. The professor also noted that the final product would not have been nearly of the same quality without such dedication. Furthermore, the professor stated that the potential publication would help in the professor's upcoming tenure review, whereas the graduate student did not have as much to gain by being the lead author.

COMMENTS: There is no doubt that, in this situation, the graduate student involved was in need of and did receive help. Being without a dissertation advisor in the last year of one's graduate program of study has serious financial, emotional, and employment consequences. Thus, the professor provided a valuable service to the student, and even went out of the way to make sure that the student's dissertation was of the highest quality.

The professor, as all professors in student/professor relationships, held a superior position to the graduate student based on status, knowledge, and experience. However, by asking the student to agree before the fact to work on turning the student's research into a publishable manuscript, the professor's actions might be seen as subtle coercion and ethically questionable in nature. Had the professor revealed the true intent of the agreement, i.e., to use the student's work as a way to further the professor's own career and not necessarily that of the student's, there is little question that the action would be considered unethical.

Furthermore, the fact that the professor worked independently of the student after the dissertation was completed to produce a manuscript and placed the professor's name first is clearly a violation of substandard 6.3 because the professor only assisted in bringing the student's project to completion. The professor did not do the original research; but only directed the dissertation project to closure—something expected of professors in doctoral granting institutions. It might have been appropriate for the professor to be listed as a second coauthor of the manuscript but such an arrangement should have been made after the graduate student and professor talked and agreed on such an arrangement.

6.4 Marriage and family therapists who are the authors of books or other materials that are published or distributed do not plagiarize or fail to cite persons to whom credit for original ideas or work is due.

VIGNETTE: A professor was well intentioned in signing a book contract for an MFT text. However, because the professor took on too many service assignments at the university and still had daily family obligations, this professor became not only stretched thin but also stressed. As the months passed, only a limited amount of work was done on the proposed text. When summer came, the professor realized there were only two months left to finish the book or publication would be delayed for another year. If publication were delayed, the publisher would ask for a return of the advance money on the book, which the professor had already spent. Therefore, the professor focused renewed attention on writing. A week before the book was due, however, it was still not finished, despite these efforts. There was one chapter left on the treatment of eating disorders. About to search the literature on the subject, the professor remembered a web site that sold research papers. When the source was checked, there were several papers on treating eating disorders from an MFT perspective. They were modifiable for the book. Thus, the professor downloaded them and integrated the material into the last chapter.

COMMENTS: A number of factors need to be considered in this case. First, the professor, mostly through no personal fault, became stretched thin and stressed out shortly after signing a book contract. These conditions affected the professor's ability to function at an optimal level, but they do not, in and of themselves, justify unprofessional or unethical behaviors. Second, the fact that time was running out does not excuse the actions taken. Third, the professor knowingly consulted a questionable source of scholarship and bought papers from that source (thereby implicitly supporting it), and then modified these materials without giving credit to where they were obtained in the hope that what was produced would be seen as original scholarship. In all of these events, the professor was in error.

Although giving back a monetary advance and waiting up to a year longer for the project to be completed could have been embarrassing and somewhat humiliating for the professor, such actions would have been far superior to the professor's claiming credit for someone else's work.

6.5 Marriage and family therapists who are the authors of books or other materials published or distributed by an organization take reasonable precautions to ensure that the organization promotes and advertises the materials accurately and factually.

VIGNETTE: Using a modified version of a well-known theory, an MFT professor wrote a unique book on working with families. The publisher of the material was most excited about the professor's book and wanted to get maximum publicity for it. Therefore, the professor was asked to fill out a form highlighting the strengths and uniqueness of the work, and to give the names of colleagues who might critique the text and provide testimonials for the book's back cover. The professor joyfully completed this task in a timely manner. Several months later, the professor received an advanced copy of the book. On the back cover was a description of the contents of the book that overstated the effectiveness of what the author had done. The therapist was mortified but felt helpless to correct the situation because the book had already gone to press.

COMMENTS: In this situation, the professor could be described as a "victim" of an over-enthusiastic publisher who was trying to gain as much exposure as possible for the new text. The publisher had a financial stake in recovering what had been invested in the publishing process and wanted the book to enhance the reputation of the publishing house too. The professor was cooperative in this endeavor, but the therapist had not exercised due diligence by checking with the publisher about the content and emphasis of planned publicity.

Since the book was published by the time the author discovered what had happened, there was a limit to what could be done. However, several options were open for addressing the situation. First, the author could have asked the publisher to modify advertising for the book to make sure it accurately portrayed the contents of the book. Such a scenario might mean that the publisher would have to pull advertisement in journals or periodicals already in press, or re-advertise the book correctly and point to the fact that the first ads were in error. Second, the author could have written an "open letter" to the AAMFT magazine and other professional organization publications where the book would be advertised and explain what happened and what the contents of the book actually were. This kind of open letter would have allowed potential readers to know that the author was aware of the mistake made and was apologetic for it having happened. Third, the author could have asked that a new jacket for the book be designed and used. While such a procedure would delay the distribution of the text and would have a cost associated with it, the reputation of the author and the publishing house would be saved and the benefits to both of them, as well as to consumers, would be enhanced.

All of these procedures could have been done in combination too. In such a way, everyone would have benefited. As previously implied, authors of publications need to exercise due diligence before a work is published to make sure the work is described accurately. Such procedures include asking for a copy of the publicity to be used in promoting the text and making corrections before the publicity and the book go to press.

6.6. Marriage and family therapists participate in activities that contribute to a better community and society, including devoting a portion of their professional activity to services for which there is little or no financial return.

VIGNETTE: In order to help socially disadvantaged residents in a large city, a local chapter of AAMFT decided to open a free MFT clinic based on the model of free legal clinics. The steering committee of the chapter figured that such a clinic would improve the mental health and marital/family functioning of this underserved population. When a member of the chapter called to solicit clinicians, one asked what the personal payoff would be. Upon hearing that benefit was in the form of helping strengthen couple and family life within the community and was thus intangible, the clinician declined the request to participate and provide services in any way. The clinician further stated that with a full-time practice, trying to do one more professional activity would hamper the quality of service to families to which there was already a commitment.

COMMENTS: Clinical MFT professionals have a lot of demands on their time. They must make a living in an environment where there is considerable competition and uncertainty about client flow and financial rewards. Therefore, it is understandable that they may be limited in what they can do for others on a pro bono basis. It is impossible to accept all requests.

However, it is important to give back to a community in gratitude for what it has provided and in order to strengthen it. Such work may involve a variety of services such as working with couples and families who cannot afford services, speaking to public groups such as PTAs about matters related to family health and well being, or lending a hand as a worker in such family-oriented projects as Habitat for Humanity. In the preceding vignette, the clinician did not feel any obligation to help those less fortunate or in need. Rather, this clinician reasoned that working with others in the free clinic would hurt the practice the therapist had already established.

The actions of the clinician in this case are not unethical per se. After all, professionals cannot do everything asked of them and this clinician may have already been committed to a number of families before being asked to help with this project. However, a pattern of refusing to assist others outside of one's immediate practice or obligations, by doing pro bono work for example, will most likely find a therapist isolated, jaded, and unfortunately out of touch with the environment and the profession of marriage and family therapy. Consistent omissions of this nature are ethically questionable.

6.7 Marriage and family therapists are concerned with developing laws and regulations pertaining to marriage and family therapy that serve the public interest, and with altering such laws and regulations that are not in the public interest.

VIGNETTE: A piece of federal legislation on mental health provided governmental reimbursement for "core providers." Within the bill were a number of recognized mental health service providers but not marriage and family therapists. An AAMFT division president, who was also a practicing MFT therapist, was alerted to the situation and quickly joined in working with the national organization to urge other clinicians to write, telephone, and personally contact their congressional representatives to have marriage and family therapists included in the bill. After the legislation passed, another professional specialist accused the division president of conflict of interest since the president had supported and urged the support by others of a bill that could help MFT's professionally and financially.

COMMENTS: Contrary to the accusation made by the fellow professional, the AAMFT division president acted ethically and in accordance with principle 6.7. The therapist was not seeking an individual advantage but was rather advocating for a specialty area—couple and family therapy—that would have been excluded from the bill if this clinician and others had not taken action. Had the exclusion taken place, couples and families needing help with situational and developmental problems would most likely not have received it from adequately educated providers. Indeed, they may have received the wrong kind of treatment. Thus, the AAMFT division president acted in the public good and for the right reasons.

6.8 Marriage and family therapists encourage public participation in the design and delivery of professional services and in the regulation of practitioners.

VIGNETTE: A community mental health services board was being established to assess what services were being provided in the community and how those services could be enhanced. Two marriage and family therapists were included on the board along with members of various other mental health specialties. As the meeting was being called to order, one of the MFTs noted the absence of anyone other than treatment providers. The response by the chair of the community group was that trained professionals are in the best position possible to know what needs to be done in a community context and to address such matters. In justification of the board composition, the chair ended by saying: "You wouldn't ask mental patients to devise their own treatment would you?"

COMMENTS: Practitioners of marriage and family therapy and other mental health providers have a special knowledge that allows them to provide needed services. However, they also have an obligation to make sure that the services they deliver are in the best interest of everyone. Part of the way therapists can be sure they are fulfilling this obligation is to solicit advice and input from others outside of their discipline, i.e., the public. Consumers of services are in an excellent position to give feedback to professionals about what the professionals are doing well and what could be done better.

In the situation described in this vignette, the MFT who spoke up was ethically justified in being concerned that persons from the public domain were not included on the board. If they were, the board would be stronger both internally and externally. The board would be perceived as a group truly interested in community welfare. It would have enhanced credibility and, more important, it would be more representative of the community it was seeking to service. The feedback provided by community representatives would be unique and could ultimately change the way mental health services were delivered.

PRINCIPLE VII FINANCIAL ARRANGEMENTS

Henry Harder, Ed.D.

9

PRINCIPLE VII FINANCIAL ARRANGEMENTS

Marriage and Family Therapists make financial arrangements with clients, third-party payors, and supervisees that are reasonably understandable and conform to accepted professional practices.

7.1 Marriage and Family Therapists do not offer or accept kickbacks, rebates, bonuses, or other remuneration for referrals; fee-for-service arrangements are not prohibited.

VIGNETTE: An MFT is part of a group practice and is involved in some business consulting on a part-time basis. The therapist is very effective in the business consulting and is frequently approached to provide referrals. This loss of revenue opportunities is a source of frustration. In discussion with the group practice partners it is suggested that others in the group see the clients, and they will pay the therapist a percentage of every hour billed. Thus the therapist still makes some money and does not lose the entire revenue opportunity, and the group practice benefits as well.

COMMENTS: It is not uncommon for an MFT to work in both clinical and non-clinical settings, such as business consulting. When in another environment it is possible that one is asked to make recommendations for where someone may go for some help. While it may be frustrating to give away business and the attendant income, a suggestion for a referral must not be based on what benefits the MFT or other MFT colleagues. MFTs must always consider what is in the best interest of the person(s) asking for assistance when making a referral. Further, given the above vignette and the frustration with losing potential revenue, it is possible that the therapist's judgment may be impaired. Consequently, this therapist should refrain from making referrals.

7.2 Prior to entering into the therapeutic or supervisory relationship, Marriage and Family Therapists clearly disclose and explain to clients and supervisees: (a) all financial arrangements and fees related to professional services, including charges for cancelled or missed appointments; (b) the use of collection agencies or legal measures for non-payment; and (c) the procedure for obtaining payment from the client, to the extent allowed by law, if payment is denied by the third-party payor. Once services have begun, therapists provide reasonable notice of any changes in fees or other charges.

VIGNETTE: An MFT had been seeing a couple for marital therapy. The couple had insurance. The initial financial arrangement was that the couple paid the therapist directly and then submitted the receipt to their insurance company for reimbursement. The insurance company then reimbursed the couple 80% of the hourly rate. After several months of this arrangement the couple told the therapist that they were experiencing financial hardship and asked for their insurance company to be billed directly. Reluctantly, after conferring with the insurance company and the couple agreeing to pay the 20% difference, the therapist agreed. Treatment went on and was eventually terminated with everyone satisfied with the progress the couple had made. Due to processing delays at the insurance company payments were far behind and accounts were not rectified until several months after treatment completion. At that time, the therapist sent the couple a reminder and several more as the couple never paid. Eventually, a collection agency was contacted and given the account. Not long after, the therapist received a very angry phone call from the couple expressing surprise at this action and threatening to launch an ethics complaint.

COMMENTS: The therapist is on weak ground here. Best practice would have been to include in the consent form used to document the informed consent to treatment process, a clear statement of what the fees for service are, what the payment expectations are and what happens if fees are not paid. If a collection agency is to be used this should also be stated. If clients' financial circumstances change partway through therapy, best practice would be to clearly document what arrangements have been made and what the repayment expectations are. It is important that clients clearly understand what they are agreeing to, what their obligations are, and what the MFT will do if they do not meet their obligations. The process is best handled through a written agreement placed in the client's file.

7.3 Marriage and Family Therapists give reasonable notice to clients with unpaid balances of their intent to seek collection by agency or legal recourse. When such action is taken, therapists will not disclose clinical information.

VIGNETTE: An MFT had seen a married couple for therapy, and sent them several notices regarding an unpaid balance. Upon hearing nothing from the clients, the case was referred to a collection agency according to the policy that was clearly outlined in the informed consent process. An issue in the case had been physical violence, specifically spousal abuse, and there was concern that someone from the collection agency may be placed at risk. Consequently, the therapist indicated in the referral that the couple had been in treatment as a result of physical abuse and that agency staff should be careful in dealing with this couple.

COMMENTS: While the therapist was well meaning and had the safety of others at heart, this was clearly a violation of client confidentiality. MFTs must first always protect the confidentiality of the client which normally includes the fact that the person is even in treatment. The code here specifically refers to "clinical information" from which we can assume that it is recognized that client identity must be revealed in order to pursue a bad debt. This does not give the therapist the right to reveal any other information. Furthermore, the clients had made no threats against third parties that might (depending on the law) trigger a "duty to protect," and collection agencies no doubt have their own procedures to protect themselves from harm.

7.4 Marriage and Family Therapists represent facts truthfully to clients, third-party payors, and supervisees regarding services rendered.

VIGNETTE: An MFT was on contract to provide services to referrals from a government agency. This agency did not pay for missed appointments and the hourly fee was less than the therapist's normal hourly rate. Clients referred from this agency did not reliably attend sessions, and when they did attend they were difficult to keep in the session. The therapist developed the practice of letting the clients leave after half an hour, while billing the agency for a full hour. Several of the clients required documentation of their hours of therapy for court purposes. The therapist recorded each session as an hour of therapy, rationalizing that they were getting as much done in half an hour and that it was more productive than keeping the client for the full hour.

COMMENTS: The therapist is not being truthful about the services being rendered. The clients do not know that the therapist is billing for a full hour and only seeing them for half an hour. They also do not know that their records will show a full hour of treatment. The agency believes that they are paying for a full hour of therapy. The issue of the efficacy of treatment is moot. The therapist is committing fraud, and more significantly, placing the clients at risk, as the information provided may be used in a court of law while it may not be meeting the letter of the law—on a court order for example. The therapist needs to be truthful about the amount of therapy being provided. The needs of the clients come first.

7.5 Marriage and Family Therapists ordinarily refrain from accepting goods and services from clients in return for services rendered. Bartering for professional services may be conducted only if: (a) the supervisee or client requests it; (b) the relationship is not exploitive; (c) the professional relationship is not being distorted; and (d) a clear written contract is established.

VIGNETTE: An MFT has been seeing a client for several months. Finances have been an issue and both parties have agreed to accrue the balance and pay off the debt over time. One day the therapist notices that the client arrives driving an older car that the therapist very much admires. The therapist suggests that the client give the car in lieu of payment. Initially the client balks at the suggestion, but eventually agrees and signs over the car. When therapy concludes, the client states that the therapist owes the client some money because the car is worth more than the amount of therapy provided.

COMMENTS: The therapist is clearly in the wrong because of section (a) of the subprinciple. However, even if the client had suggested this arrangement, it still would have been problematic. The monetary value of the car was never independently assessed, nor mutually agreed upon, and as a result, this arrangement could have been exploitative for either party. Further, if one party or the other had been worried about being exploited, then the professional relationship would have been distorted. An MFT must never initiate bartering. If the client had initiated the suggestion, best practice would have been to suggest selling the car and using the money acquired to pay for therapy. This would have left control in the hands of the client. Alternatively, and less desirably, the car's value could have been assessed by an independent professional assessor, and the value so established could have been applied to the cost of therapy. Such an arrangement would need to be clearly documented in order to protect the best interests of the client and the therapist.

7.6 Marriage and Family Therapists may not withhold records under their immediate control that are requested and needed for a client's treatment solely because payment had not been received for past services, except as otherwise provided by law.

VIGNETTE: An MFT has been providing court-mandated therapy to a couple with the goal of helping them communicate. The financial arrangement is that they pay all the fees 50/50. The therapist is required to produce several reports for the courts over the course of treatment. Two months before the end of the mandated treatment one party of the couple stops paying, pleading financial hardship. Upon discussion, it becomes apparent that both parties of the couple have run out of money. The therapist agrees that therapy will continue until the end of the mandated time and that they can pay off their debt in installments. One party of the couple makes a great effort to pay off the debt and does so over several months. The other party makes no attempt to pay off the debt. Six months after treatment the therapist receives a request from both parties to write a summary treatment report because they have begun treatment with another therapist. Writing the report would require an hour of time. Because one party still owes money and probably would not pay their share for the new report, the therapist refuses the request. The couple then asks instead for copies of the existing reports that had been previously submitted to the court. Again the therapist refuses, citing the overdue balance.

COMMENTS: This subprinciple alludes to therapists' ethical duty to continue to act in the clinical best interests of former clients. From a business standpoint, marriage and family therapists certainly have the right to pursue payment for services rendered. When payment is past due, legitimate means for seeking collection include legal action and collection agencies, as long as reasonable notice has been provided as required by subprinciples 7.2 and 7.3. When a client who owes fees makes a request for clinical records, therapists may see this as an opportunity to obtain some leverage in the struggle to obtain payment and may therefore be tempted to make fulfillment of the client's request contingent upon payment of the debt. When it is foreseeable that doing so could harm the clinical best interests of a former client because the records are needed for the former client's current care, subprinciple 7.6 bars that tactic. When in doubt, it would be wise to err in the direction of providing the clinical records, while continuing to use other legitimate means to resolve the debt.

In the preceding vignette, the therapist's refusal to grant the couple's first request may be ethically defensible because in requesting a new report the couple were asking for additional professional services (the hour or so of report writing). Compliance with subprinciple 7.6 does not require therapists to write new, additional clinical records for a client who has reneged on paying for previous services. However, when the therapist refused to simply send along copies of existing reports, this definitely crossed into the realm of a violation, given the clear relevance of the records to the couple's current treatment.

PRINCIPLE 8 ADVERTISING

Travis E. Martin, M.H.S.

Raquel Anaya Muller, M.A.

10

Frederick J. Katz III, Ed.S.

PRINCIPLE VIII: ADVERTISING

Marriage and family therapists engage in appropriate informational activities, including those that enable the public, referral sources, or others to choose professional services on an informed basis.

8.1 Marriage and family therapists accurately represent their competencies, education, training, and experience relevant to their practice of marriage and family therapy.

VIGNETTE: The therapist received a call from a couple requesting therapy to address serious problems in their marriage. They asked about the therapist's credentials. The therapist indicated having specialization in all areas of marital therapy. As the discussion continued, the couple specified that they were having difficulties communicating in several areas of their relationship. Again, the therapist assured them that any problems they were having could be handled in therapy. By the third session, the therapist realized that the couple's problems were primarily based around their sexual relationship. This was beyond the therapist's scope of competency; however, treatment was continued without supervision for several more sessions. The couple soon realized that the therapist was not able to deal with their sexual problems and that they had more knowledge about sexuality in general than the therapist did. The couple confronted the therapist regarding the matter and the therapist acknowledged having only a limited knowledge of sexuality. They felt betrayed and angry because of the therapist's misrepresentation. They decided to file a complaint with AAMFT.

COMMENTS: In this case, the therapist falsely claimed to be competent in all areas of marital therapy. The therapist should have provided a more specific description of the therapist's knowledge and qualifications. The therapist could have avoided this pitfall and been more helpful to the couple by doing one of the following: 1) Explain that the therapist was not competent in sex therapy, but would seek supervision if the couple would like to continue treatment; 2) Provide them a referral for a qualified sex therapist; or 3) Refer the couple to an MFT with more experience working with sexual issues.

8.2 Marriage and family therapists ensure that advertisements and publications in any media (such as directories, announcements, business cards, newspapers, radio, television, Internet, and facsimiles) convey information that is necessary for the public to make an appropriate selection of professional services. Information could include: (a) office information, such as name, address, telephone number, credit card acceptability, fees, languages spoken, and office hours; (b) qualifying clinical degree (see subprinciple 8.5); (c) other earned degrees (see subprinciple 8.5) and state or provincial licensures and/or certifications; (d) AAMFT clinical member status; and (e) description of practice.

VIGNETTE: The therapist had recently moved to a new location and decided to advertise in the local yellow pages, as well as to get new business cards printed. The advertising stated that the therapist was bilingual (English–Spanish). Two different Spanish-speaking individuals called for services, and appointments were made. When individuals arrived, they each found out that the only person who spoke Spanish was the office assistant. Further, the therapist failed to tell both clients that the Spanish-speaking office assistant was also a therapist in training who could assist in translating during sessions. One client felt comfortable enough speaking English, and received excellent services. Another left therapy after the first session, angry and disillusioned, and then refused to seek treatment from any other therapists.

COMMENTS: The ethical violation in this case lies in the therapist's inaccurately advertising as a bilingual therapist in both the yellow pages and on the business cards. The advertisements should have indicated that the office assistant/therapist in training—not the therapist—spoke Spanish. In addition, each Spanish-speaking client could have been given the option of allowing the assistant, who was a therapist in training, to sit in as a translator in the sessions.

8.3 Marriage and family therapists do not use names that could mislead the public concerning the identity, responsibility, source, and status of those practicing under that name, and do not hold themselves out as being partners or associates of a firm if they are not.

VIGNETTE: The therapist, a master's level licensed clinician who practiced under the name EST Family Services, leased office space from EST Psychology Associates. EST Psychology Associates, a group of all licensed psychologists, had an excellent reputation in the community and had been recognized for its contributions to the mental health field. When a client called to make an appointment, the telephone was answered as "EST," leading the client to believe that the therapist was associated with EST Psychology Associates. Being aware of EST's excellent reputation, the client chose to see the therapist, despite the hefty fee, later learning that EST Family Services was not affiliated with EST Psychology Associates. In spite of having received good treatment, the client felt betrayed at having been led to believe that the therapist was a psychologist and was part of the very prestigious group. Furthermore, the client's decision to pay a higher fee was based on the reputation of EST Psychology Associates, of which the therapist was not a part. The client filed a complaint with the state and AAMFT.

COMMENTS: In this case, it is clear that the therapist employed a misleading advertisement, which led the client to make a poorly informed decision. Moreover, the therapist used the fact of leasing space from the prestigious firm and using a similar name to charge more money. The therapist and EST Family Services staff should have made it clear from the start that they were not a part of EST Psychology Associates, despite the fact that they were located in the same office. In addition, clients should have been solely charged on the merits of their therapist's expertise, and not at the expense of other therapists' reputation.

8.4 Marriage and family therapists do not use any professional identification (such as a business card, office sign, letterhead, Internet, or telephone or association directory listing) if it includes a statement or claim that is false, fraudulent, misleading, or deceptive.

VIGNETTE: A family decided to go for a family evaluation at ABC agency, basing their decision on information they had seen on the agency's Web page indicating that it ascribed to the philosophies and training of a certain MFT theorist. Upon completion of the evaluation session, the therapist who had conducted the evaluation gave the family a business card, which stated the same information as the Web page. The clients took this to mean that this therapist was also trained in this particular theory, since they had not only seen this information on the Web page, but also on the therapist's business card. The therapist did not have much experience using the theory to which ABC agency ascribed. This fact became evident after a couple of sessions. The family, feeling mislead, filed a complaint with both AAMFT and the state licensing board.

COMMENTS: The Web page suggested that the agency subscribed to a specific MFT theory. Based on that, the family decided to seek an evaluation at this agency. They made an appointment under the assumption that the therapist subscribed to the same principles. At the end of the first evaluation session, the therapist gave the family a business card, which confirmed the assumption about the therapist's theoretical orientation. The therapist should have made clear that the theoretical orientation was different from that of the agency, and should not have used a business card that implied false information. The therapist also had a responsibility to bring to the agency's attention that the information on the Web page and business cards was, indeed, incorrect.

8.5 In representing their educational qualifications, marriage and family therapists list and claim as evidence only those earned degrees: (a) from institutions accredited by regional accreditation sources recognized by the United States Department of Education; (b) from institutions recognized by states or provinces that license or certify marriage and family therapists; or (c) from equivalent foreign institutions.

VIGNETTE: A master's level licensed marriage and family therapist in private practice recently received a Ph.D. degree from a non-accredited university. The therapist proceeded to use the title "Dr." and advertised as such through new letterhead and business cards. This implied that the therapist had earned a doctorate from an appropriately accredited institution of higher education.

COMMENTS: Though the therapist had clearly earned a Ph.D., the fact that this degree was not awarded by an accredited institution means that there was a misrepresentation of academic credentials, and therefore the public was misled through false advertisement and self-promotion.

8.6 Marriage and family therapists correct, wherever possible, false, misleading or inaccurate information and representations made by others concerning the therapist's qualifications, services, or products.

VIGNETTE: The community mental health agency that an MFT, Morgan, worked for, stated in its literature that it provided an extensive family-based substance abuse program. The licensed MFT that ran the program left for another job. The agency hired another therapist who did not have a substance abuse background. However, the clinic continued to advertise the program for several months and continued to get referrals. A colleague notified Morgan that the agency continued to advertise the family-based substance abuse program, though no such service was being offered. Morgan put those concerns in writing to the administration and the advertisements were modified.

COMMENTS: Inaccurate information, whether deliberate or unintentional, can mislead both the public and other mental health care providers. This often results in clients having their expectations unmet and other agencies referring clients for services that do not exist. In this case, first, the newly hired MFT should have brought the false advertisement to the agency's attention. Had a complaint been filed, both the new MFT and the agency would have been accountable. Morgan clearly did the right thing by contacting the agency. Morgan could have filed a complaint against the new MFT for misrepresentation of credentials and could have filed a complaint with the state/province licensing board about the agency's false advertisement.

8.7 Marriage and family therapists make certain that the qualifications of their employees or supervisees are represented in a manner that is not false, misleading, or deceptive.

VIGNETTE: The director of a well-respected mental health agency promoted it as having the majority of its clinicians licensed as MFTs. The agency had ten full-time clinicians, of who three were licensed as MFTs. The director anticipated that five of the therapists who had completed their hours and were waiting to take the national exams would be licensed within the next few weeks. However, the agency came up for review by one of the state certification bodies, and was found to have misleading information regarding the agency's licensed staff. The agency was found to be in violation and the director was reprimanded.

COMMENTS: Even though those five therapists were eventually licensed, the director committed an ethical violation by claiming that the agency staff met a certain standard of competency that they had not yet met. This is misleading to both clients and other mental health agencies on which the clinic relied for referrals. This may result in referrals that cannot be serviced and clients whose expectations and needs are not met. The director should have waited until the non-licensed clinicians were licensed before promoting their qualifications. In addition, this kind of information could have permanently damaged a good agency's reputation.

8.8 Marriage and family therapists do not represent themselves as providing specialized services unless they have the appropriate education, training, or supervised experience.

VIGNETTE: A therapist, looking to expand into new practice areas, went to a few seminars on gay relationships, and began advertising as a sex counselor with specialization in gay relationships without having met the criteria from the American Association of Sex Educators, Counselors, and Therapists (AASECT). These advertisements led to many referrals, the majority of which were gay couples. These gay couples went to the therapist expecting a specific level of expertise. Several couples inquired about the therapist's credentials and found that the therapist was neither certified as a sex counselor, nor associated with AASECT in any way. More than one client made an official complaint to the AAMFT.

COMMENTS: A therapist should not mistake a few seminars for specialized competency. In this case, there is a specific level of specialization, which comes from the certifying body AASECT. Only that association can make the designation of "sex counselor." While this therapist may have had some exposure to gay and lesbian issues through seminars, this did not meet the level of specialized service. Therefore, the therapist should not have self-promoted as having specialized experience in this particular area. The consequences of making such false claims ranged from clients' expectations not being met, and needs not being fulfilled, to causing major damage to both the individuals and the couple. The therapist could have advertised more generally to build a practice, worked toward AASECT certification, and then advertised as a sex counselor.

APPENDIX A - AAMFT CODE OF ETHICS - EFFECTIVE JULY 1, 2001

PREAMBLE

The Board of Directors of the American Association for Marriage and Family Therapy (AAMFT) hereby promulgates, pursuant to Article 2, Section 2.013 of the Association's Bylaws, the Revised AAMFT Code of Ethics, effective July 1, 2001.

The AAMFT strives to honor the public trust in marriage and family therapists by setting standards for ethical practice as described in this Code. The ethical standards define professional expectations and are enforced by the AAMFT Ethics Committee. The absence of an explicit reference to a specific behavior or situation in the Code does not mean that the behavior is ethical or unethical. The standards are not exhaustive. Marriage and family therapists who are uncertain about the ethics of a particular course of action are encouraged to seek counsel from consultants, attorneys, supervisors, colleagues, or other appropriate authorities.

Both law and ethics govern the practice of marriage and family therapy. When making decisions regarding professional behavior, marriage and family therapists must consider the AAMFT Code of Ethics and applicable laws and regulations. If the AAMFT Code of Ethics prescribes a standard higher than that required by law, marriage and family therapists must meet the higher standard of the AAMFT Code of Ethics. Marriage and family therapists comply with the mandates of law, but make known their commitment to the AAMFT Code of Ethics and take steps to resolve the conflict in a responsible manner. The AAMFT supports legal mandates for reporting of alleged unethical conduct.

The AAMFT Code of Ethics is binding on Members of AAMFT in all membership categories, AAMFT-Approved Supervisors, and applicants for membership and the Approved Supervisor designation (hereafter, AAMFT Member). AAMFT members have an obligation to be familiar with the AAMFT Code of Ethics and its application to their professional services. Lack of awareness or misunderstanding of an ethical standard is not a defense to a charge of unethical conduct.

The process for filing, investigating, and resolving complaints of unethical conduct is described in the current Procedures for Handling Ethical Matters of the AAMFT Ethics Committee. Persons accused are considered innocent by the Ethics Committee until proven guilty, except as otherwise provided, and are entitled to due process. If an AAMFT Member resigns in anticipation of, or during the course of, an ethics investigation, the Ethics Committee will complete its investigation. Any publication of action taken by the Association will include the fact that the Member attempted to resign during the investigation.

PRINCIPLE I - RESPONSIBILITY TO CLIENTS

Marriage and family therapists advance the welfare of families and individuals. They respect the rights of those persons seeking their assistance, and make reasonable efforts to ensure that their services are used appropriately.

1.1. Marriage and family therapists provide professional assistance to persons without discrimination on the basis of race, age, ethnicity, socioeconomic status, disability, gender, health status, religion, national origin, or sexual orientation.

1.2 Marriage and family therapists obtain appropriate informed consent to therapy or related procedures as early as feasible in the therapeutic relationship, and use language that is reasonably understandable to clients. The content of informed consent may vary depending upon the client and treatment plan; however, informed consent generally necessitates that the client: (a) has the capacity to consent; (b) has been adequately informed of significant information concerning treatment processes and procedures; (c) has been adequately informed of potential risks and benefits of treatments for which generally recognized standards do not yet exist; (d) has freely and without undue influence expressed consent; and (e) has provided consent that is appropriately documented. When persons, due to age or mental status, are legally incapable of giving informed consent, marriage and family therapists obtain informed permission from a legally authorized person, if such substitute consent is legally permissible.

1.3 Marriage and family therapists are aware of their influential positions with respect to clients, and they avoid exploiting the trust and dependency of such persons. Therapists, therefore, make every effort to avoid conditions and multiple relationships with clients that could impair professional judgment or increase the risk of exploitation. Such relationships include, but are not limited to, business or close personal relationships with a client or the client's immediate family. When the risk of impairment or exploitation exists due to conditions or multiple roles, therapists take appropriate precautions.

1.4 Sexual intimacy with clients is prohibited.

1.5 Sexual intimacy with former clients is likely to be harmful and is therefore prohibited for two years following the termination of therapy or last professional contact. In an effort to avoid exploiting the trust and dependency of clients, marriage and family therapists should not engage in sexual intimacy with former clients after the two years following termination or last professional contact. Should therapists engage in sexual intimacy with former clients following two years after termination or last professional contact, the burden shifts to the therapist to demonstrate that there has been no exploitation or injury to the former client or to the client's immediate family.

1.6 Marriage and family therapists comply with applicable laws regarding the reporting of alleged unethical conduct.

1.7 Marriage and family therapists do not use their professional relationships with clients to further their own interests.

1.8 Marriage and family therapists respect the rights of clients to make decisions and help them to understand the consequences of these decisions. Therapists clearly advise the clients that they have the responsibility to make decisions regarding relationships such as cohabitation, marriage, divorce, separation, reconciliation, custody, and visitation.

1.9 Marriage and family therapists continue therapeutic relationships only so long as it is reasonably clear that clients are benefiting from the relationship.

1.10 Marriage and family therapists assist persons in obtaining other therapeutic services if the therapist is unable or unwilling, for appropriate reasons, to provide professional help.

1.11 Marriage and family therapists do not abandon or neglect clients in treatment without making reasonable arrangements for the continuation of such treatment.

1.12 Marriage and family therapists obtain written informed consent from clients before videotaping, audio recording, or permitting third-party observation.

1.13 Marriage and family therapists, upon agreeing to provide services to a person or entity at the request of a third party, clarify, to the extent feasible and at the outset of the service, the nature of the relationship with each party and the limits of confidentiality.

PRINCIPLE II - CONFIDENTIALITY

Marriage and family therapists have unique confidentiality concerns because the client in a therapeutic relationship may be more than one person. Therapists respect and guard the confidences of each individual client.

2.1 Marriage and family therapists disclose to clients and other interested parties, as early as feasible in their professional contacts, the nature of confidentiality and possible limitations of the clients' right to confidentiality. Therapists review with clients the circumstances where confidential information may be requested and where disclosure of confidential information may be legally required. Circumstances may necessitate repeated disclosures.

2.2 Marriage and family therapists do not disclose client confidences except by written authorization or waiver, or where mandated or permitted by law. Verbal authorization will not be sufficient except in emergency situations, unless prohibited by law. When providing couple, family or group treatment, the therapist does not disclose information outside the treatment context without a written authorization from each individual competent to execute a waiver. In the context of couple, family or group treatment, the therapist may not reveal any individual's confidences to others in the client unit without the prior written permission of that individual.

2.3 Marriage and family therapists use client and/or clinical materials in teaching, writing, consulting, research, and public presentations only if a written waiver has been obtained in accordance with Subprinciple 2.2, or when appropriate steps have been taken to protect client identity and confidentiality.

2.4 Marriage and family therapists store, safeguard, and dispose of client records in ways that maintain confidentiality and in accord with applicable laws and professional standards.

2.5 Subsequent to the therapist moving from the area, closing the practice, or upon the death of the therapist, a marriage and family therapist arranges for the storage, transfer, or disposal of client records in ways that maintain confidentiality and safeguard the welfare of clients.

2.6 Marriage and family therapists, when consulting with colleagues or referral sources, do not share confidential information that could reasonably lead to the identification of a client, research participant, supervisee, or other person with whom they have a confidential relationship unless they have obtained the prior written consent of the client, research participant, supervisee, or other person with whom they have a confidential relationship. Information may be shared only to the extent necessary to achieve the purposes of the consultation.

Principle III – Professional Competence and Integrity

Marriage and family therapists maintain high standards of professional competence and integrity.

3.1 Marriage and family therapists pursue knowledge of new developments and maintain competence in marriage and family therapy through education, training, or supervised experience.

3.2 Marriage and family therapists maintain adequate knowledge of and adhere to applicable laws, ethics, and professional standards.

3.3 Marriage and family therapists seek appropriate professional assistance for their personal problems or conflicts that may impair work performance or clinical judgment.

3.4 Marriage and family therapists do not provide services that create a conflict of interest that may impair work performance or clinical judgment.

3.5 Marriage and family therapists, as presenters, teachers, supervisors, consultants and researchers, are dedicated to high standards of scholarship, present accurate information, and disclose potential conflicts of interest.

3.6 Marriage and family therapists maintain accurate and adequate clinical and financial records.

3.7 While developing new skills in specialty areas, marriage and family therapists take steps to ensure the competence of their work and to protect clients from possible harm. Marriage and family therapists practice in specialty areas new to them only after appropriate education, training, or supervised experience.

3.8 Marriage and family therapists do not engage in sexual or other forms of harassment of clients, students, trainees, supervisees, employees, colleagues, or research subjects.

3.9 Marriage and family therapists do not engage in the exploitation of clients, students, trainees, supervisees, employees, colleagues, or research subjects.

3.10 Marriage and family therapists do not give to or receive from clients (a) gifts of substantial value or (b) gifts that impair the integrity or efficacy of the therapeutic relationship.

3.11 Marriage and family therapists do not diagnose, treat, or advise on problems outside the recognized boundaries of their competencies.

3.12 Marriage and family therapists make efforts to prevent the distortion or misuse of their clinical and research findings.

3.13 Marriage and family therapists, because of their ability to influence and alter the lives of others, exercise special care when making public their professional recommendations and opinions through testimony or other public statements.

3.14 To avoid a conflict of interests, marriage and family therapists who treat minors or adults involved in custody or visitation actions may not also perform forensic evaluations for custody, residence, or visitation of the minor. The marriage and family therapist who treats the minor may provide the court or mental health professional performing the evaluation with information about the minor from the marriage and family therapist's perspective as a treating marriage and family therapist, so long as the marriage and family therapist does not violate confidentiality.

3.15 Marriage and family therapists are in violation of this Code and subject to termination of membership or other appropriate action if they: (a) are convicted of any felony; (b) are convicted of a misdemeanor related to their qualifications or functions; (c) engage in conduct which could lead to conviction of a felony, or a misdemeanor related to their qualifications or functions; (d) are expelled from or disciplined by other professional organizations; (e) have their licenses or certificates suspended or revoked or are otherwise disciplined by regulatory bodies; (f) continue to practice marriage and family therapy while no longer competent to do so because they are impaired by physical or mental causes or the abuse of alcohol or other substances; or (g) fail to cooperate with the Association at any point from the inception of an ethical complaint through the completion of all proceedings regarding that complaint.

PRINCIPLE IV – RESPONSIBILITY TO STUDENTS AND SUPERVISEES

Marriage and family therapists do not exploit the trust and dependency of students and supervisees.

4.1 Marriage and family therapists are aware of their influential positions with respect to students and supervisees, and they avoid exploiting the trust and dependency of such persons. Therapists, therefore, make every effort to avoid conditions and multiple relationships that could impair professional objectivity or increase the risk of exploitation. When the risk of impairment or exploitation exists due to conditions or multiple roles, therapists take appropriate precautions.

4.2 Marriage and family therapists do not provide therapy to current students or supervisees.

4.3 Marriage and family therapists do not engage in sexual intimacy with students or supervisees during the evaluative or training relationship between the therapist and student or supervisee. Should a supervisor engage in sexual activity with a former supervisee, the burden of proof shifts to the supervisor to demonstrate that there has been no exploitation or injury to the supervisee.

4.4 Marriage and family therapists do not permit students or supervisees to perform or to hold themselves out as competent to perform professional services beyond their training, level of experience, and competence.

4.5 Marriage and family therapists take reasonable measures to ensure that services provided by supervisees are professional.

4.6 Marriage and family therapists avoid accepting as supervisees or students those individuals with whom a prior or existing relationship could compromise the therapist's objectivity. When such situations cannot be avoided, therapists take appropriate precautions to maintain objectivity. Examples of such relationships include, but are not limited to, those individuals with whom the therapist has a current or prior sexual, close personal, immediate familial, or therapeutic relationship.

4.7 Marriage and family therapists do not disclose supervisee confidences except by written authorization or waiver, or when mandated or permitted by law. In educational or training settings where there are multiple supervisors, disclosures are permitted only to other professional colleagues, administrators, or employers who share responsibility for training of the supervisee. Verbal authorization will not be sufficient except in emergency situations, unless prohibited by law.

PRINCIPLE V - RESPONSIBILITY TO RESEARCH PARTICIPANTS

Investigators respect the dignity and protect the welfare of research participants, and are aware of applicable laws and regulations and professional standards governing the conduct of research.

5. 1 Investigators are responsible for making careful examinations of ethical acceptability in planning studies. To the extent that services to research participants may be compromised by participation in research, investigators seek the ethical advice of qualified professionals not directly involved in the investigation and observe safeguards to protect the rights of research participants.

5. 2 Investigators requesting participant involvement in research inform participants of the aspects of the research that might reasonably be expected to influence willingness to participate. Investigators are especially sensitive to the possibility of diminished consent when participants are also receiving clinical services, or have impairments which limit understanding and/or communication, or when participants are children.

5.3 Investigators respect each participant's freedom to decline participation in or to withdraw from a research study at any time. This obligation requires special thought and consideration when investigators or other members of the research team are in positions of authority or influence over participants. Marriage and family therapists, therefore, make every effort to avoid multiple relationships with research participants that could impair professional judgment or increase the risk of exploitation.

5.4 Information obtained about a research participant during the course of an investigation is confidential unless there is a waiver previously obtained in writing. When the possibility exists that others, including family members, may obtain access to such information, this possibility, together with the plan for protecting confidentiality, is explained as part of the procedure for obtaining informed consent.

PRINCIPLE VI - RESPONSIBILITY TO THE PROFESSION

Marriage and family therapists respect the rights and responsibilities of professional colleagues and participate in activities that advance the goals of the profession.

6.1 Marriage and family therapists remain accountable to the standards of the profession when acting as members or employees of organizations. If the mandates of an organization with which a marriage and family therapist is affiliated, through employment, contract or otherwise, conflict with the AAMFT Code of Ethics, marriage and family therapists make known to the organization their commitment to the AAMFT Code of Ethics and attempt to resolve the conflict in a way that allows the fullest adherence to the Code of Ethics.

6.2 Marriage and family therapists assign publication credit to those who have contributed to a publication in proportion to their contributions and in accordance with customary professional publication practices.

6.3 Marriage and family therapists do not accept or require authorship credit for a publication based on research from a student's program, unless the therapist made a substantial contribution beyond being a faculty advisor or research committee member. Coauthorship on a student thesis, dissertation, or project should be determined in accordance with principles of fairness and justice.

6.4 Marriage and family therapists who are the authors of books or other materials that are published or distributed do not plagiarize or fail to cite persons to whom credit for original ideas or work is due.

6.5 Marriage and family therapists who are the authors of books or other materials published or distributed by an organization take reasonable precautions to ensure that the organization promotes and advertises the materials accurately and factually.

6.6 Marriage and family therapists participate in activities that contribute to a better community and society, including devoting a portion of their professional activity to services for which there is little or no financial return.

6.7 Marriage and family therapists are concerned with developing laws and regulations pertaining to marriage and family therapy that serve the public interest, and with altering such laws and regulations that are not in the public interest.

6.8 Marriage and family therapists encourage public participation in the design and delivery of professional services and in the regulation of practitioners.

Principle VII - Financial Arrangements

Marriage and family therapists make financial arrangements with clients, third-party payors, and supervisees that are reasonably understandable and conform to accepted professional practices.

7.1 Marriage and family therapists do not offer or accept kickbacks, rebates, bonuses, or other remuneration for referrals; fee-for-service arrangements are not prohibited.

7.2 Prior to entering into the therapeutic or supervisory relationship, marriage and family therapists clearly disclose and explain to clients and supervisees: (a) all financial arrangements and fees related to professional services, including charges for canceled or missed appointments; (b) the use of collection agencies or legal measures for nonpayment; and (c) the procedure for obtaining payment from the client, to the extent allowed by law, if payment is denied by the third-party payor. Once services have begun, therapists provide reasonable notice of any changes in fees or other charges.

7.3 Marriage and family therapists give reasonable notice to clients with unpaid balances of their intent to seek collection by agency or legal recourse. When such action is taken, therapists will not disclose clinical information.

7.4 Marriage and family therapists represent facts truthfully to clients, third-party payors, and supervisees regarding services rendered.

7.5 Marriage and family therapists ordinarily refrain from accepting goods and services from clients in return for services rendered. Bartering for professional services may be conducted only if: (a) the supervisee or client requests it, (b) the relationship is not exploitative, (c) the professional relationship is not distorted, and (d) a clear written contract is established.

7.6 Marriage and family therapists may not withhold records under their immediate control that are requested and needed for a client's treatment solely because payment has not been received for past services, except as otherwise provided by law.

Principle VIII - Advertising

Marriage and family therapists engage in appropriate informational activities, including those that enable the public, referral sources, or others to choose professional services on an informed basis.

8.1 Marriage and family therapists accurately represent their competencies, education, training, and experience relevant to their practice of marriage and family therapy.

8.2 Marriage and family therapists ensure that advertisements and publications in any media (such as directories, announcements, business cards, newspapers, radio, television, Internet, and facsimiles) convey information that is necessary for the public to make an appropriate selection of professional services. Information could include: (a) office information, such as name, address, telephone number, credit card acceptability, fees, languages spoken, and office hours; (b) qualifying clinical degree (see subprinciple 8.5); (c) other earned degrees (see subprinciple 8.5) and state or provincial licensures and/or certifications; (d) AAMFT clinical member status; and (e) description of practice.

8.3 Marriage and family therapists do not use names that could mislead the public concerning the identity, responsibility, source, and status of those practicing under that name, and do not hold themselves out as being partners or associates of a firm if they are not.

8.4 Marriage and family therapists do not use any professional identification (such as a business card, office sign, letterhead, Internet, or telephone or association directory listing) if it includes a statement or claim that is false, fraudulent, misleading, or deceptive.

8.5 In representing their educational qualifications, marriage and family therapists list and claim as evidence only those earned degrees: (a) from institutions accredited by regional accreditation sources recognized by the United States Department of Education, (b) from institutions recognized by states or provinces that license or certify marriage and family therapists, or (c) from equivalent foreign institutions.

8.6 Marriage and family therapists correct, wherever possible, false, misleading, or inaccurate information and representations made by others concerning the therapist's qualifications, services, or products.

8.7 Marriage and family therapists make certain that the qualifications of their employees or supervisees are represented in a manner that is not false, misleading, or deceptive.

8.8 Marriage and family therapists do not represent themselves as providing specialized services unless they have the appropriate education, training, or supervised experience.

This Code is published by: American Association for Marriage and Family Therapy

112 South Alfred Street – Alexandria, VA 22314-3061

703-838-9808 – 703-838-9805 FAX – www.aamft.org

Violations of this code should be brought in writing to the attention of:

AAMTF Ethics Committee

112 South Alfred Street

Alexandria, VA 22314-3061

Telephone: 703-838-9808

Email: ethics@aamft.org

APPENDIX B - ADDITIONAL ETHICS RESOURCES FROM THE AMERICAN ASSOCIATION FOR MARRIAGE AND FAMILY THERAPY

· Visit the American Association for Marriage and Family Therapy (AAMFT) website at *http://www.aamft.org*. There you will find the full text of the *AAMFT Code of Ethics*, and information about how ethical complaints are filed and processed.

· *http://www.FamilyTherapyResources.net* is a service of the American Association for Marriage and Family Therapy. At this site, you will find a searchable database of books, conference tapes, articles, fact sheets, and upcoming conferences. Many of these resources address ethical and legal issues in the practice of family therapy.

· Even the most ethically conscious clinician will experience ethical and legal quandaries. Hence, the AAMFT Legal Risk Management Plan was created as a free benefit of AAMFT membership. Through this program members can access numerous legal and ethical fact sheets, and consult with an attorney via telephone about legal matters relating to their professional practice. AAMFT members can also request a free ethical advisory opinion based on the *AAMFT Code of Ethics* and the experience of the AAMFT Ethics Committee. Professional liability insurance is available to AAMFT members at a group rate.